Tales from

RIDING HOUSE STREET

A faded London house and the Cypriots who lived in it

Helen Evangelou

First published in Great Britain in 2018 in paperback form and ebook form

A CIP catalogue record for this book is available from the British Library

ISBN 978 1 9164223 0 8 (B format)
ISBN 978 1 9164233 1 5 (ebook format)

Typeset in Bembo by RefineCatch Limited, Bungay, Suffolk
Printed and bound in Great Britain by Clays Ltd, Elcograf S.p.A

www.ridinghousestreet.co.uk
@TalesfromRHS

For my parents
Photis and Vasilou
In gratitude

CONTENTS

Welcome to London	1
The Beginning	4
On the Map	18
Our House	25
House Mates	35
Local Heroes	43
Celebrations	51
Liquid Gold	56
Chief Mouser	62
Flying the Flag	66
Kids in the City	72
Family Restaurants	87
The Glory	98
Down the Aisle	104
Pratt Street	114
The Beautiful Game	122
Pocket Money	129
The Doctor and the Dentist	131
Language and Learning	135
High School	139

Rag Trade Friends 145
Family Holidays 147
Jo's Flight 160
Back to Roots 165
Anglo Akanthou Aid Society 186
Greeks on Film 195
Oxford Street and Beyond 199
The Food of Love 206
Career Girl 217
The F Word 240
And In The End 246
Acknowledgements 261

WELCOME TO LONDON

Me? I'm from the West End. Not any old West End, but the West End in the greatest city in the world – London. Our house was located just north of Oxford Circus, a stone's throw from Regent Street and the BBC's Broadcasting House. Growing up in the 1950s and 60s, I saw the city morph from wartime monochrome into dazzling colour. Mine was a childhood full of laughter, despite a life lived in relative hardship in a faded Georgian house shared with three other Cypriot families - and with only one outside loo.

I lived there until I got married in 1976. There were a lot of cousins, a lot of gatherings and always a lot of food. They say a family that eats together stays together, and that for us was so true. Our family extended to half of London, or so it seemed, and the table in our basement kitchen always heaved with relatives and friends. My mother used to say that we were like honey and people constantly swarmed around our beehive.

My parents were Greek Cypriot migrants who were proud of their heritage and made sure I spoke Greek before I spoke

English. They had me dressing up in traditional costume to recite poems at the after-hours Greek school, just so I could understand my roots. Arriving from Cyprus pre-war in the mid-1930s, my parents found life in their new country exciting but tough. They had left behind their family, their much-loved ancestral land and their village, which was so remote it took them many hours to travel to the nearest town. But they were hardworking and tenacious, with what could be an infuriatingly philosophical acceptance of just about anything life threw their way.

I was born in St Mary's, Paddington, and my first outing as a tiny baby was to Regent's Park, wheeled there by my proud mother after a quick hello to Camden's Greek Orthodox Church. The park would become my second home, a welcome relief from our cramped and gloomy rooms and the tiny backyard. But, as bleak as it was, our house rang with life and with characters so colourful I sometimes wondered whether I'd made them up. There was Panagis, the "tough guy" on the floor above, whose yelling could be heard halfway down the street but who would go to bed wearing a hair net to protect his quiff. Or Panos, the boy on the top floor who, when he was older, threatened to drop poison gas over Cyprus unless its government paid him an extortionate amount of money.

Perhaps the best thing about the house was its location and its proximity to, well, just about everything. Theatres, cinemas, restaurants and shops were all within easy walking distance, as well as music venues such as the 100 Club and the Marquee. Then again, if we felt lazy there was not one but seven nearby tube stations to choose from. London was the world's greatest city, buzzing with energy and life, and I was living right in the centre of its beating heart.

This is my story, of being the daughter of migrants who came from Cyprus to the UK, and of growing up through the years of political upheaval in both countries.

THE BEGINNING

Not many people get to grow up in central London, but I lived there, in the same house, for more than 25 years, through to the mid-70s. Our home was on Riding House Street, three blocks north of Oxford Street, at no. 57, an old Georgian house with peeling burgundy paint and black railings. The street's unusual name is a reference to a military riding academy that stood there in the early 18th century. Originally called Riding House Lane, it ran from Langham Place to the west to Great Titchfield Street to the east, beyond which it became Union Street. In 1937, the whole thoroughfare was renamed Riding House Street and so it remains to this day. Until recently, you could see a ghost sign of the name Union Street on the corner wall with Cleveland Street.

My parents, Photis Evangelou and Vasilou Ktori, were Greek Cypriot. Dad was fair-skinned with hazel eyes and chestnut hair, and could easily have passed for a German. Mum, on the other hand, was dark: her olive skin would turn a deep brown within five minutes of sitting in the sun. They came from a small village in the north of Cyprus called

Akanthou, set beneath the Kyrenia range of mountains. Dad, out of desperation to save his family's ancestral home and the many acres of land they owned, came to the UK in 1934. His objective was to pay off a debt his landowner father, Hadji-Yiannis, had amassed after years of drought and also crippling taxes imposed by the ruling British, with a view to returning to Cyprus once his family was solvent. Mum, as it turned out, was to follow a few years later.

Cyprus had been leased by the British from the Ottomans by mutual consent in 1878. The deal was that Britain would protect the Ottomans against any Russian aggression in return for Britain ensuring the defence of the Suez Canal, where they had assumed an interest. In 1914, the British annexed the island after Turkey sided with the Germans during World War I, and it became a British Crown colony in 1925.

The Ottomans had ruled Cyprus for some 400 years. Its multiple occupiers before that had included the Assyrians, Persians, Romans and Venetians, who were no doubt attracted to its vast wealth in copper. The metal's extraction can be traced back to 4000 BC and it is where the island gets its name: Kypros, meaning copper. Strategically placed on the map, Cyprus is undoubtedly also a listening post for the troubled Middle East, and was once branded an 'unsinkable aircraft carrier' by the US politician Henry Kissinger. The island finally gained independence from Britain in 1960, after a five-year guerrilla war aimed initially at uniting it with Greece, a campaign called "enosis" (union).

Cyprus had a mixed population but was predominantly Greek Cypriot, tracing its Greek roots back to the Hellenisation of the island around 1200 BC. Greek Cypriots made up 80% of the 600,000 population; another 18% were Turkish Cypriots, with Armenians and Maronites the remaining 2%. This cultural mix got on relatively well, until fighting broke out between the two main communities in 1963 and feelings were soured.

But this was the 1930s and Dad, aged 24, was embarking on a trip into the unknown. As it turned out, his early life in the UK was no joyride; in fact, it was downright miserable. Accompanied by his closest friend – Tata (Godfather) Elias, who was also Mum's first cousin – he arrived in London to find hunger and despair, worse than any deprivation back home in Cyprus. It was 1934 and his new country was deep in the Depression. There were hardly any jobs and no money. Dad would tell stories of how he and Tata Elias resorted to eating out of dustbins, and of surviving a house fire in Charlotte Street after which all they had left were the clothes they stood in.

Things got so bad that they decided to risk it and look for jobs further afield – they had nothing to lose. They had heard about an Athenian Greek who operated cargo ships out of Cardiff, so they scraped together some money and set off on the train to the Welsh port. Upon arrival they were offered work, but not before the Greek seized their passports. They were now tied to him, the paymaster and the slaves.

And slave work it was. Dad was given a job as a stoker, shovelling coal into the ship's furnace. Tata Elias was somewhat better off and worked up above as a deck hand. Despite the hardships, life on the *Aghia Thalassini* (St Seafarer) was bearable, sometimes even enjoyable, and they visited exotic locations from Africa to Brazil. Years later, Dad was to say that Rio, with its Sugarloaf Mountain, was the most beautiful place he had ever set eyes on.

My parents remained engaged, but three years on there was no sign of Dad returning to Cyprus. Mum was getting worried and a neighbour kept putting suspicious thoughts into her head: Dad was a man on his own, after all, and could be getting up to no good. As if. I don't think Dad so much as looked at another woman in the 60 years my parents were together, but the seed of doubt had been sewn.

Fidelity wasn't the only thing worrying Mum. Greeks are naturally superstitious and one day she spotted an owl sitting in a tree. "Please God, don't let it fly over me," she prayed. Some Greeks, Mum being one of them, believe that if an owl flies over you then you might as well be dead, such is the amount of bad luck that will be heaped on you. Of course, the cursed thing did fly over. She went home and cried all night, praying that her beloved Photis was alive and safe.

Around the time of the owl incident, while Dad was at sea shovelling coal, he slipped and almost fell into the mouth of the furnace. Instinctively, he reached out and grabbed a nearby fixed ladder. "Panaghia mou!" he cried, calling out to the Virgin Mary. "Save me!" And saved he was. When my parents were eventually reunited, he told Mum of his near miss. She knew straight away it was the fault of the owl and loathed the sight of them forever after.

But, back in Cyprus, Mum had decided enough was enough. She was going to the UK and no one was going to persuade her otherwise. Saying goodbye to her distraught parents, she boarded the ship from Limassol and sailed to England, to her new life and her husband-to-be. By then, Dad had returned from his seafaring adventures, with his passport safely in hand.

It took three weeks for Mum to get to the UK and soon after that my parents were married. That was in 1938. By 1939, Mum was pregnant with my sister – and then, with luckless timing, World War II broke out. Like a lot of migrants in those days they had moved to the West End, because that's where the jobs were. And for 50 years that was where they lived, in the area they loved best. Years later, often after visiting relatives in leafy Richmond, Mum would get off the bus at Oxford Circus and breathe a sigh of relief: "Eneshi san to youest en" (There's nowhere like the West End).

Throughout the war years my parents lived in central London, apart from nine months spent in Sutton, Surrey. Dad wasn't called up because he was classified unfit: he had a wound on his leg from a dog bite in Cyprus that kept weeping and bleeding, so he was considered unsuitable, aka category C. Tata Elias, Uncle Michael (Mum's brother) and Uncle Photis (Mum's cousin) all served and they hated it. To escape the bombing, my parents moved out of London. They chose to go to Sutton in 1943, where they ran a restaurant and thought they would be safer. Safer? I don't think so. The restaurant was frequently filled with drunken Canadian soldiers, who often tried to rob Dad and once tried to kill him. Mum was so terrified they would manhandle my three-year-old sister that she would hide her under the stairs until closing time. "Where's the kid?" the soldiers would ask when they walked in.

Despondent, they returned to London nine months later. Dad got a job as a kitchen porter in a Cypriot-owned restaurant, the Glory, on Goodge Street, while Mum looked after my sister at home in Riding House Street, occasionally doing tailoring work. When the sirens sounded, she would pick up my sister with one hand, a bag of baby things and a torch with the other, and run to the underground shelters of Warren Street and Goodge Street. When she emerged, she wouldn't know whether Dad was alive or dead. Amazingly, they all survived.

Dad, seated left, with friends, Akanthou, 1913

This Certificate is not a Passport. [illegible]

CYPRUS.

Nº 29655

Certificate of British Nationality

Granted under the Cyprus (Annexation) Orders in Council, 1914 to 1929.

I, Herbert Richmond Palmer, Knight Commander of the Most Distinguished Order of Saint Michael and Saint George, Commander of the Most Excellent Order of the British Empire, Governor and Commander-in-Chief of the Colony of Cyprus, hereby certify that:

Photis Hajı Yianni Haji Photi Haji Evangelou

of whom a description, photograph and specimen signature appear on this certificate, has become a British Subject under and by virtue of the Cyprus (Annexation) Orders in Council, 1914 to 1929.

DESCRIPTION.

Profession Farmer

Place and Date of Birth Akanthou, Cyprus, 1910.

Height: 5 feet 6 inches

Forehead Regular Eyes Hazel

Nose Regular Mouth Regular

Chin Round Colour of Hair [illegible]

Complexion Fair Face Oval

Any special peculiarities Nil

PHOTOGRAPH.

SIGNATURE.

[illegible]

In witness whereof I have hereto subscribed my name this ... day of September 1934

By His Excellency's Command.

[illegible signature]

Colonial Secretary.

Dad's ID card issued in 1934 by the British colonial administration when he emigrated from Cyprus

Aboard the "Aghia Thalassini" Dad is third from left, Tata Elias is fifth from left

En route to England with a stopover at the Acropolis, Athens. Mum in white, second from left. Aunty Vass is standing, far left

Κτήματα ὑφιστάμενα ἐν τῷ ὑποθήκῃ κατὰ τὴν ἡμερομηνίαν τῆς ἐκδόσεως τῆς παρούσης φόρμας.

Τίτλος 'Αριθμός	Ἡμερομηνία Ἐγγραφῆς	Χωρίον	Τοποθεσία	Εἶδος Κτήματος	Μερ.	Σκ.	Πρ.	Τ.Π.
13106	1/10/30	'Ακανθοῦ	Τραχῶνι	Χωράφι	ὅλον	9	-	-
13107	"	"	"	(23 χαρ.4 ἐλιές	"			
24605	"	"	Λαξιά Παπαδιάς	5 ἐλιές	"			
24604	"	"	" "	Χωράφι	"	2	-	-
24589	"	"	Σκάλα τοῦ "Μαρτῆ	"	"	1	3	-
24590	"	"	" " "	3 ἐλιές	"			
14449	"	"	Βούκκα τοῦ Φωτινοῦ	Χωράφι	"	2	-	-
14450	"	"	" " "	6 ἐλιές	"			
30310	"	"	'Αγκαθερή	Χωράφι	"	2	1	-
30311	"	"	"	2 ἐλιές	"			
30298	"	"	'Αθκιάκι	Χωράφι	"	3	2	-
30299	"	"	"	2 ἐλιές	"			
28679	"	"	Πλάτσες	Χωράφι	"	4	2	-
28680	"	"	"	2 ἐλιές	"			
15009	"	"	Πέρα Μάνδρα	Χωράφι	"	4	1	-
15010	"	"	" "	3 χαρουπιές	ὅλο			
27140	"	"	Καμκί	Χωράφι	ὅλον	3	-	-
27141	"	"	"	6 χαρουπιές	"			
29535	"	"	Μαυρόνορος	Χωράφι	"	5	1	-
29536	"	"	"	(2 ἐλιές,1 χαρουπ	"			
12787	"	"	Βουνός	Χωράφι	"	9	1	-
12788	"	"	"	(12 ἐλιές,6 χαρουπ	"			
12798	"	"	Τρουλ.ιά	Χωράφι	"	-	3	900
12799	"	"	"	3 ἐλιές	"			
12869	"	"	Βουνός	Χωράφι	"	1	1	-
12870	"	"	"	4 ἐλιές	"			
12997	"	"	"	Χωράφι	"	4	-	-
12998	"	"	"	(11 χαρουπ,2 ἐλιές	"			
25429	"	"	Κάψαλος	Χωράφι	"	4	1	-
25430	"	"	"	7 χαρουπιές	"			
4875	"	"	Τουμασίνα	Χωράφι	"	9	1	-
4876	"	"	"	22 ἐλιές	"			
4900	"	"	"	Χωράφι	"	2	3	-
4901	"	"	"	(3 ἐλιές,1 χαρουπ	"			
22581	"	"	Γρουσούκκι	Χωράφι	"	9	3	-
22582	"	"	"	8 χαρουπιές	"			
17581	"	"	Βουναρούδια	Χωράφι	"	2	2	-
17582	"	"	"	(19 ἐλιές,1 χαρουπ	"			
12355	"	"	Χωραφερή	Χωράφι	"	6	-	-
12356	"	"	"	(11 ἐλιές,10 χαρουπ	"			
12357	"	"	"	Χωράφι	"	6	-	-
12358	"	"	"	16 χαρουπιές	"			
12386	"	"	"	Χωράφι	"	3	-	-
12387	"	"	"	28 χαρουιές	"			
12265	"	"	"	Χωράφι	"	2	-	-
12266	"	"	"	(17 ἐλιές,2 χαρουπ	"			
12351	"	"	"	Χωράφι	"	-	-	2300
12352	"	"	"	2 ἐλιές	"			
12176	"	"	Κατσούρας	1 χαρουπιά	"			
12177	"	"	Βουνός	Χωράφι	3/24	18	-	-
12186	"	"	Κατσούρας	"	ὅλον	1	-	-
12187	"	"	"	(3 ἐλιές,1 χαρουπ	"			

ἀκολουθεῖ

The deeds to some of Dad's land in Akanthou, itemising his olive and carob trees (registered in 1925)

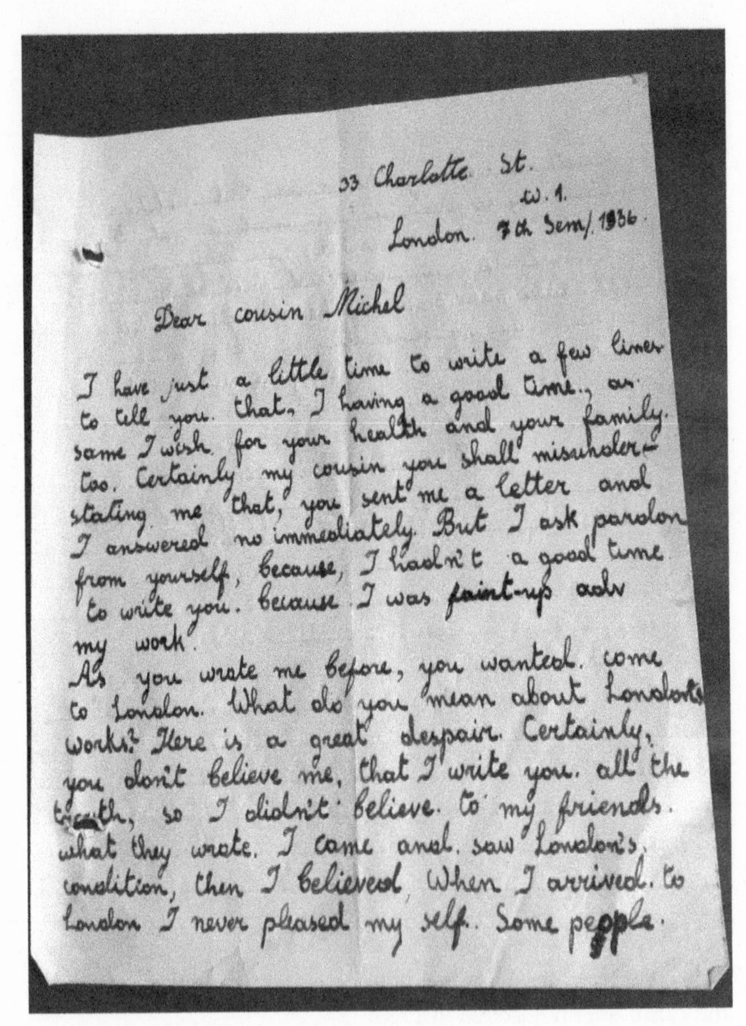

33 Charlotte St.
W. 1.
London. 7th Sem/. 1936.

Dear cousin Michel

I have just a little time to write a few lines
to tell you. that, I having a good time., as
same I wish for your health and your family.
too. Certainly my cousin you shall misunder-
stating me that, you sent me a letter and
I answered no immediately. But I ask pardon
from yourself, because, I hadn't a good time
to write you. because I was faint-up adv
my work.
As you wrote me before, you wanted. come
to London. What do you mean about London's
works? Here is a great despair. Certainly,
you don't believe me, that I write you. all the
truth, so I didn't believe. to my friends.
what they wrote. I came and. saw London's
condition, then I believed. When I arrived. to
London I never pleased my self. Some people.

Dad's letter to his cousin Micheli in Akanthou, written in his 'best' English. He describes his despair in London, but nevertheless offers to help

somethere arausing themselves, but not I.
Well my cousin If you want to come here
write me other letter. you may rely upon me.
Excouse me. If my letter full of mistake;
I have not been in the school. but all.
teach by my ~~selve~~ self.
Kind regards to every.one member. of.
your family

I remain your. sincere. cousin.

Chotiy

Uncle Michael and Tata Elias in British Army uniforms

My sister, Jo, aged about eight, photographed at All Souls Primary School

Me, aged two

ON THE MAP

At the eastern end of Riding House Street stands All Souls C of E Primary School, rebuilt in its present form in 1908, with its front entrance on Foley Street. The school was founded in 1824 and was originally housed in cottages and stables next to All Souls Church, at the other end of the street. Still open today, All Souls has always been full of children from different ethnic backgrounds. For me, it's a place of happy memories, though I suppose some of them are filtered through rose-tinted glasses.

All Souls Church, by the architect John Nash, first opened its doors in 1824. Generally, if you went to All Souls Primary you also attended All Souls Church. As children, we would amble two by two up Riding House Street from the school to the church, for weekly services and to celebrate religious festivals. Each of us would be given violets on Mother's Day to take home to our mums; in the autumn, at Harvest Festival, our mums would give whatever they could afford – marrows, apples and tinned fruit. Every year I go back to All Souls, with my sister and some old primary school friends, for the annual Christmas carols. For us, it's a renewal, an anchoring.

As well as the two All Souls there was the hospital, the Middlesex. This red-brick Victorian hulk, built in 1891, took up an entire block, spanning Cleveland, Mortimer, Nassau and Riding House streets. For our family, momentous events took place in that hospital. My sister, Joanna, was born there in 1939, three months after the war broke out. Dad died there in 1989. Mum had a mastectomy and two hip replacements there. But I wasn't born at the Middlesex, because for some reason Mum was told she couldn't give birth to more than one child in the same hospital. She was rushed across London to St Mary's in Paddington, some four miles away, even though we lived within touching distance of the Middlesex maternity ward.

By strange coincidence, my husband, Tim, was also born in St Mary's. I've no idea how that came about as his parents lived in East London. Fast-forward to the 80s and to the song *West End Girls* by the Pet Shop Boys. It makes me smile when I hear the lyrics celebrating "East End boys and West End girls" – it's as though they were written with us in mind.

The Middlesex was "our" hospital, but it also nursed some rather famous people. Sir Winston Churchill was admitted in 1962 after breaking a leg in Monte Carlo, and the writer Rudyard Kipling died there in 1936. For us, there were visits whenever we got sick or when a Cypriot relative dragged us along to act as their interpreter. I was lucky because that job usually fell to my sister, who was 10 years older than me. Mum would stand over her and make her do it; she spent hours in that hospital while everyone else was out playing. Lucky Jo!

There was a day, many years later, when the hospital was targeted by one of my high-spirited journalist colleagues.

Walking back to ITN after a rather liquid lunch at the Glory, he decided to practise his bowling with a bread roll taken from the restaurant. He aimed it at one of the Middlesex's open windows and hurled it as hard as he could. We never knew where it landed, or even on whom it landed, but we giggled at the thought like naughty schoolchildren.

To our horror, the hospital was demolished in 2008. The site was acquired by the Candy brothers and for years it lay undeveloped, like a huge gaping wound. The effect on us was visceral. Eventually, the site was bought by the property company Exemplar and a vast block of luxury flats was built. It has been renamed Pearson Square, I presume after the architect JL Pearson, who designed the hospital chapel. At the time of writing, a studio flat is selling for more than £1 million. The chapel, which gave comfort to so many people in times of sorrow, has listed status so has been retained, but its present use is as a wedding and music venue (the term dancing on one's grave comes to mind). Surprisingly, the facade on Nassau Street has also been kept, perhaps because the name Middlesex Hospital is engraved across the front and the developers felt it would give the place some historical kudos. For me, the new-build is a ghastly temple to Mammon, one of many now blighting our urban landscape.

In the early 60s, the Victorian clothing factories over the road from us were pulled down and eventually replaced in 1969 by a large modern building that housed ITN, the national TV news organisation (15 years later, I ended up working there). As if having one TV news station on our street wasn't enough, at the other end, next to All Souls Church, stood the BBC's Broadcasting House. The fabulous art deco building first opened in 1932 and since then shiny new extensions have been added. Alas, and to the consternation of local bars and restaurants, ITN moved to Gray's Inn Road in 1990. In those days, journalists and cameramen spent hours in restaurants and pubs enjoying a drink or three. "If you want me, beep me" was the instruction to those of us left behind on the news desk, though to their credit, when a story broke they would be on it, often all day and all night.

None of the houses in our street had gardens. We all had backyards, which was where the dustbins lived, and there was an occasional window box but little other greenery. To more than compensate, we had Regent's Park – in my view, the most glorious of all city parks. That was where we spent every spare weekend and most of our school holidays. The park was a good 10-minute walk from our house and as kids we were taken along for "fresh air" and to "release our energy", as Mum would say. I suppose I appreciated it then, but probably not nearly as much as I do now. Regent's Park is a beautiful oasis like no other.

Me (left) and Sooty on the corner of Riding House and Candover streets, 1963. Middlesex hospital is behind us on the right

Dad in his favourite coat outside our house, 57 Riding House Street

Painting of Christ at All Souls Church, Langham Place

Aerial photo (taken from GPO tower) of the demolished Middlesex hospital. The Grade II listed Chapel is untouched

OUR HOUSE

It is thought that no. 57 was built around 1725. The house is still standing, although it had quite a radical makeover in the 1980s, when it was gutted and its facade retained. No. 57 had, and still has, four storeys and a basement. My parents moved there in 1943 after stints in Berwick Street and Fitzroy Street and their nine months in Sutton; they initially rented the three rooms on the first floor and later took over the basement. Another family lived on the ground floor, so you could say our accommodation was a bit like a sandwich and someone else was the filling.

The first floor had a sitting room at the front that doubled as my sister's bedroom. Next to that was a narrower room, the kitchen, with my parents' bedroom at the back. Until the age of five I slept in a cot in my parents' room, but for reasons of privacy they eventually moved me out. At that point they decided to renovate the basement, creating a new kitchen and putting me and Jo in what was the old kitchen. So it remained until my sister moved out in 1967 and I left to get married in 1976.

Life was hard, especially for Mum. Her original kitchen had

no running water and she was constantly climbing up to the landing between the first and second floors, where there was a corner basin with a cold tap. Keeping warm was a nightmare – we were always freezing. We had coal fires back then and Mum would have to go down into the cellar to fill up her buckets with fuel. The ordeal usually fell to her as Dad's job as a chef meant he worked long, unsociable hours and wasn't there when we were awake. We used to call him the lodger because we only saw him on his day off on Sundays, or his half day on Thursdays.

Things improved when my parents took over the basement, but we were still always cold. There were two rooms down there, one of which was used by Mum and her Cypriot friend Tallou as a tailoring workshop. That room, at the front, was converted into the kitchen, but the back room remained a junk store until much later, when we turned it into a bathroom. I remember a wonderful old kitchen range that my parents pulled out and threw away. It would probably be worth a small fortune now, but back then "all that old stuff" took too much time and money to maintain, so the range was replaced by a two-bar electric fire that my mother thought was a godsend.

Wash day must have been hellish, especially when Mum took on a "part-time" job (full-time minus 45 minutes) just off Bond Street, hand-finishing suits for Harvey Nichols and Harrods. We had no washing machine or mangle so everything had to be laundered by hand – Mum's only concession was the sheets, which she took to the laundry over the road. Monday was whites day; Tuesday, coloureds. To dry the clothes, Dad ran some rope along the ceiling of the basement hallway and along the open well of the basement, alongside the coal cellars. In those dank conditions it's a wonder anything ever dried.

Mum stuck with the same job until she retired some 40 years later, but the pension she received was minimal as her boss hadn't paid national insurance on her behalf and she hadn't been savvy enough to ask. There was a lot of wishing him to hell after she left, and we like to think that Hades is indeed where his mean-spirited bones ended up. The only upside for Mum was that she was able to buy, before they were dispatched to Knightsbridge, some wonderful suits at a reasonable price for my sister. Jo always looked fabulous in them and was the envy of her friends.

Before our renovations at no. 57 there was only one toilet, shared by four families. It was outside in the yard, where there was no electricity and, of course, no heating. We used to light a candle to see and would sit on the toilet hoping the resident spiders wouldn't fall on our heads or, even worse, into our knickers. It was freezing cold most of the time, so you had to finish quickly and get back inside before you turned blue. In the early years we all kept chamber pots in our bedrooms, but once I moved in with my sister she became quite stroppy and demanded I use the outside loo. To add to the misery, the communal stair lights were switched off at 11pm, so God help you if you wanted to pee after that time. In the middle of the night and shivering with cold, I'd have to get out of bed, light a candle and find my way downstairs. On top of that, I would be paralysed with fear because I thought the house was haunted. One night I freaked when a warm, furry object brushed past my legs. Fortunately, I realised it was just our cat prowling around – he could see me but I couldn't see him.

Weekly bath time was a military operation and, of course, Mum was the one who did all the work. The tin bath would be brought into the kitchen and placed in front of the oven, which had its door open and the temperature turned up high. Mum would fill the bath by boiling umpteen kettles, and that would take forever. This ordeal must have tried her patience to the limit: after a long day at work all she wanted to do was put her feet up for five minutes, but instead she had this godforsaken tin bath to deal with. The only living creature who wasn't stressed by the operation was our cat, who slept on his favourite chair while the room slowly filled up with hot, steaming air. How Mum must have envied him.

Dad didn't use the tin bath – he couldn't have fitted into it even if he tried. Once a week he would take himself off to the Marshall Street baths in Soho, where he could put a coin in the slot and have a man-size tub all to himself. What did we all do between bath times? I shudder to remember. We would go into the junk room in the basement and have a washdown while standing in a basin full of hot water. What a spartan life it was. I suppose that if, like my parents, you grew up in hardship in a small village, having to fill and empty a tin bath in a kitchen wasn't such a bad deal. At my grandfather's house in Cyprus, the toilet was a hole in the dirt floor of the stables, and it wasn't a cat that looked on but the family donkey.

When Jo and I grew up, we put our foot down (had histrionics) and my parents caved in. The junk room was cleared and a new bathroom was created. It had been a long time coming, but this at last was luxury – and "fingers up" to the rest of the house, we thought! They had to make do with zero sanitation facilities, although it seemed some of them couldn't have cared less. We would watch in horror as the man on the ground floor emptied his chamber pot into the roadside drain outside the house. He was always quite open about it and didn't care who saw him.

Needless to say, it was Mum who cleaned the house from the first floor down to the basement, including the lino-covered stairs and hallway. After washing them, she would get down on her hands and knees and polish them, too. Despite this area being communal, she was the only one who cleaned it. Despina on the second floor would occasionally have a go, but she wasn't well so it was easier for Mum to just get on with it. Of course, her work also included cleaning the solitary toilet. I don't know how she coped with having to clean up everyone's crap, but that's literally what she did.

Because they had two girls, my parents always tried to make the house look as good as possible. They weren't obliged to carry out any maintenance – they were tenants, after all, or what was known back then as "controlled tenants". But the rent they paid was minimal, so the landlord never put his hand in his pocket to redecorate or carry out any refurbishment. In the mid-60s, Mum and Dad paid a decorator to paint the outside of the house and wallpaper the hall and stairway. They even bought a carpet for the stairs, a nice brown one.

The exterior of the house now looked very smart. Instead of peeling Georgian paint, the outside, up to first-floor level, was painted a respectable cream. The rest of the exterior was exposed London stock brick. Our front door was painted a glossy black and the original door knocker, a brass lion's head, gleamed. There was no doorbell, but we had our own system to discern whose visitors were at the door: people would knock once for us, twice for the residents of the second floor and three times for the third floor. Or occasionally you'd get a friend, like Yeros, shouting through the railings to my mum in the basement: "Raaa... Valisijia, ela anixe tin porta" (Hey... Valisijia [sic] come and open the door). The couple on the ground floor rarely had visitors, so they weren't included in the "system", and anyway, people could just shout through their front window, which they usually kept open. Sometimes we would get lazy, and instead of going down to open the door we would throw the keys out of the window so visitors could let themselves in. It was the same for the second and third floors. You had to be careful walking down Riding House Street from all the keys being thrown about.

With the exception of the Welsh woman on the ground floor, our house was entirely occupied by Greek Cypriots, along with no. 55 next door. Their Cypriot habits came with them. Much of the time they thought they were still living in their village back home. If they wanted to talk to a neighbour, they would stick their head out of the window and shout their name – invariably another head would emerge for a chat. On warm evenings, friends and neighbours would gather on the stoop of no. 57. They would bring their chairs and sit outside the front door, laughing and gossiping into the night while watching their kids playing on the street.

The house always felt like a commune. When you came through the front door there was never any worry that you might upset the neighbours by making too much noise. Jo and I would often sit astride the banisters and slide down them from the first floor, laughing as we fell into a heap at the bottom. Greeks love to sing and we would warble at the tops of our voices as we climbed the stairs. Adam, who lived on the second floor with his parents, had a good voice and would always break into song as he made his way upstairs; sometimes Jo and I would sing along with him through the walls.

Conversations at no. 57 were always loud. You could hear everything (well, almost) and so it felt like we all lived with each other. Adam's dad had a really loud voice: he liked to bet on the horses and every Saturday would be spent swearing or whooping at his TV. You always knew if he'd won or lost. It was exactly the same with football: you could tell how Chelsea, his team, were doing by the level and type of noise he was making.

Sometimes you heard things you wished you hadn't. One day, four-year-old Panos on the third floor was heard bellowing "poutana, poutana, poutana" (whore) at his mother. My mum, who never stood for such insolence, heard this and was horrified. Charging up the stairs, she grabbed Panos by the ear and shook him hard until he stopped. "Aren't you ashamed of yourself, calling your mother such names?" she asked. His poor mum looked at mine and shook her head: "Tell him, Mrs Vassi, he's such a handful and he never listens to a word I say." I don't think today's social services would have been very impressed with my mum.

Outside our house in the 1940s: Dad (centre) with Tata Elias (right)

In our upstairs sitting room, 1950: Mum, me, Dad and Jo

Jo outside our house

Jo with her friend Corallia on the corner of Riding House Street. Note the bollard that Adam was to fall off years later, cracking his head open

HOUSE MATES

Panos, the disrespectful boy, lived with his parents, Irini and Symeon, on the top floor. They generally kept themselves to themselves. Symeon was every inch a gentleman, very polite, so it was a mystery how they managed to breed this little brat, who was sweet but naughty and destructive. He was also highly intelligent. Panos was a handful from the start and drove his mother to despair.

As a boy of eight, Panos had many hobbies and pastimes including a keen interest in chemistry. Strange-looking parcels addressed to him would arrive from chemical companies, and hundreds of letters would pile up in the communal hallway, as though he were running a mail order business from their tiny flat. The rest of the house would worry about the contents, especially the "weird" parcels, and I remember Panagis on the second floor announcing: "Toutos o shillombastardos en an mas skotosi mian imera" (This bastard dog is going to kill us one of these days). Prophetic words, as we came to realise.

The chemistry sets proved harmless enough, but in 1987, the 37-year-old Panos got it into his head that he would blackmail the Cypriot government by threatening to gas the whole island. According to the Associated Press, Panos, under the pseudonym Commander Nemo, warned he would "wipe out all life on Cyprus" unless the government handed over US$15 million. He was arrested by anti-terrorist detectives in London after an investigation and in 1989 was tried at the Old Bailey. He received a five-year sentence and was described in court as "eccentric but devious".

The younger Panos, although wildly misguided, occasionally found himself in the right place at the right time. Our house stood in the shadow of the BT Tower, or the GPO Tower, as it was known then. At around 4.30am on 31 October 1971, I was suddenly shaken out of my bed by a deafening bang, the loudest I had heard in my life. I knew straight away that it was a bomb and it was close. There was a strange sucking sound and my bedroom window shook; I heard glass falling to the ground outside. As I lay there in shock, I heard someone racing down the stairs. The front door crashed shut and the sound of footsteps receded into the night. Upstairs, Panos had also twigged what was going on and had grabbed his camera and run. He did well. His photo was the first to be taken of the tower, believed to have been bombed by the IRA; he sold it to *The Sun* newspaper and it was then syndicated to the rest of the world. Fame, indeed, for our "eccentric but devious" neighbour.

On the second floor lived Panagis, his wife, Despina, and their young son, Adam. They were also from Cyprus, from the same village as my parents, although they came to the UK some years later. Panagis could be quite a tyrant – his friends called him Tough Guy – yet he could be charming as well. He had an opinion on everything and would let you know what it was, usually very loudly. Despina waited on him hand and foot. I would sometimes go upstairs to their flat to watch TV (we didn't have one until I was 16) and would see her fussing over his supper, usually steak. She would prepare this in the small kitchen and present it to him on a tray in the sitting room, with a folded napkin and the salt and pepper pots. If there was anything he didn't like, Despina would soon know about it. Despite his hard persona, he could sometimes be caught wearing a hair net. Jo and I would stare in disbelief, but he would shrug it off, saying it was to keep his wavy hair and particularly his quiff in place. Like a lot of seemingly hard men, his appearance was very important to him and he strutted around like a cockerel in his handmade suits and polished shoes.

Adam was a boisterous little boy who was constantly being yelled at by his dad – never more so than when he fell off a bollard while we were out playing one evening. With blood pouring out of his head and with Panagis's ire rising, Adam was dragged over to the Middlesex to get stitched up. He survived, but the memory has remained vivid and it's one of the things Adam and I still talk about.

At about the age of seven, Adam developed health problems, while his father contracted tuberculosis. Adam was sent to Cyprus to live with his grandparents in remotest Akanthou, even though he had been born in London and had never lived there. I will never forget the day he left, and the sight of his mother collapsed in our hallway, sobbing and beating her chest. Her only child was being taken away from her. She wasn't even allowed to see him off at the airport – her husband had ordered her to stay at home. Years later, in his teens, Adam returned to live with his parents in Riding House Street, continuing his studies and graduating in electrical engineering. He is now married to my first cousin Eleni and they have two boys, Pani and Paul.

On the ground floor of no. 57 were just two rooms, occupied by an elderly Greek Cypriot, George Kountis (the man with the chamber pot), his Welsh partner, Annie, and a series of corgis. Theirs seemed a strange relationship. It looked like he never worked, and he spent most of his time shuffling from one room to the other making endless cups of tea in the blackest, dirtiest kettle I'd ever seen. Mum always commented disparagingly on "to kettlo tou Kounti" and how filthy it was, but also on his rooms, which looked like a pigsty. He and Annie spent most of their time holed up in the front room, where they also slept. They did have attractive window boxes, though, full of lemon geraniums and koutalouthkia, which translates as "little spoons".

They were nice people and occasionally Annie would visit us in our bustling kitchen. She was always up for a laugh and spoke a smattering of Greek, which kept us amused. We even went on holiday together – they introduced us to the delights of caravanning and the beautiful landscape of North Wales, where we shared holidays in Llandanwg, Harlech and Penmaenmawr. Annie was also the person who broke the news to us that JFK had been assassinated. I will never forget her words: "President Kennedy's been shot." My sister and I were making our way upstairs to bed and we froze on the spot.

Our landlord, Henry Holmes, had an office where my parents went every week to pay the rent. In those days it was something like £3 a week. During the war, the landlord had offered my father the house for the princely sum of £400. Dad turned the offer down, saying he was planning to return to Cyprus where he had houses and land and, besides, who could foretell the future with German bombs raining down? Sadly for Dad, he never did go back. My parents stayed in London while my sister and I finished our education and began our careers. In 1974, a year before he was due to retire, our land and property in northern Cyprus were seized by the Turkish army after they invaded the island. Needless to say, the house in Riding House Street is now worth millions.

Our living arrangement worked quite well and we learned to make the best of it. The kitchen was the hub of our world. It was a large room with the usual freestanding cabinets, a freestanding cooker and a large oak table that opened out to accommodate half of London, or so it seemed. I marvel now at how Mum managed to look after us all. She would cook a meal from scratch every night before tackling the chores. Our home was open to all and, believe me, all did come. I'm reminded of the Beatles song *Everybody's Trying To Be My Baby* (originally sung by Carl Perkins): "Well they took some honey from a tree, dressed it up and they called it me, everybody's trying to be my baby..."

Almost every night, a friend or member of the family would call round and stay for a few hours. These people were our visitors, even if they were uninvited, so had to be treated as proper guests. A cup of tea offered on its own was anathema to Mum, and in fact to most Greeks we know. If we were eating when they came round, they would be made to eat with us, or at least forced to try biscuits and cakes. It was considered rude to carry on eating while a guest looked on and even ruder if you sat with your back to them. There's an old Cypriot saying that if you call round when someone's eating, your mother-in-law loves you. Work that one out.

I don't know how Mum conjured up meals to feed these people, especially when they turned up unannounced. At Christmas and Easter, preparations were of enormous proportions, especially at Easter, which is huge in the Orthodox calendar. Mum would fast all through Easter week and go to church every night. Then, on Easter Saturday, she would be up at 6am to prepare the traditional cheese and raisin pies (flaounes) and sesame breads. A silk sheet, woven by her in Cyprus, would be laid out across the length the kitchen floor, where she would place the many small breads she had spent hours kneading and rolling.

After coming home from church on Easter Saturday, usually at around midnight, we would all sit around the table for a bowl of avgolemoni, a traditional Greek soup of egg, lemon and rice, cooked with chicken. As well as being served at Easter, it is also "mother's medicine" and is dished out when we feel unwell and every time we come home from an overseas journey, "to settle our stomachs". It's extremely warming and more often than not does the trick.

On special occasions when we had invited guests, usually on Sundays, we would eat upstairs in the sitting room, which was transformed into a formal dining room. The tablecloth would be laid and nuts, gherkins, cucumbers, tomatoes, halloumi cheese, whatever we had, would appear. Sometimes there were treats like pickled samphire or Cypriot pork preserved in fat. Bottles of alcohol would emerge, usually

Johnnie Walker's Red Label whisky and Commandaria, a Cypriot fortified wine not dissimilar to port. There would also be bottles of beer, but rarely wine (we didn't start drinking wine in Riding House Street until the late 60s, when I started buying it). Then we would sit down to the main meal, usually avgolemoni followed by a roast and accompanied by dolmades (stuffed vine leaves) and pastichio (macaroni cheese with mince). I think about the preparation involved and wonder how Mum managed it.

It was all very well having "special guest lunches" upstairs on the first floor, but someone had to carry the food up three flights of stairs from the basement. Jo and I would help Mum lug platter after platter up the stairs, but it was usual for her not to sit with us until pudding because of all the ferrying she had to do. Dad, head of his Cypriot family, would hardly lift a finger, although he did sometimes help with the prep after he became a chef trained in French cuisine. Poor Mum: not only was she the human food lift but she was also the empty plates lift. All those dishes had to be taken back down to the kitchen, where they were washed by hand and rinsed. In those bad old days before anyone had a dishwasher, it took hours.

Adam, aged five

LOCAL HEROES

It may have been an old and decrepit house, but I loved no. 57 to bits – it was a crazy, happy place, full of laughter. Riding House Street was very colourful, offering the whole spectrum of life bang in the middle of London. Opposite our house was Jones the dairy. This was run by the elderly Mrs Jones from Wales (no one ever knew her first name) and her confirmed-bachelor son, David. From this traditional old shop you could buy a range of food as well as produce from the farm. My sister recalls the milk being ladled out from milk churns into your own bottle, but I remember the Lucozade that Mum would buy as our weekly treat.

Next door was the pub, the Green Man. For some reason, Dad didn't drink at the Green Man, and Mum never stepped foot inside a pub, preferring to drink at home and referring to beer as "katourobira tous englezous" (Englishman's piss beer). Not that she was an alcohol snob. She could down a bottle of Red Label at Christmas and had a regular glass of Commandaria before going to bed at night.

On the other side of the dairy were the snack bar and the laundry where Mum took our sheets. Down the road, next to the Green Man, was the Victorian clothing factory that made dresses and later became ITN (the building was eventually knocked down and the site is now occupied by flats). I remember the Cypriot girls knocking off work and walking down the street arm in arm, laughing and chattering as they made their way home. Opposite the factory was Rumsey's fish and chip shop, where you could buy the best cod and chips for 2/6, and a tobacconist called Williams. On the corner of Candover Street stood a wonderful building called Bouldings. Built in 1903, it has an elaborate mosaic advertisement on its side that is still there today. Opposite this, and taking up the entire block, was the dear old Middlesex.

Living opposite a dairy and a pub, you saw a lot of life. At around 3am the milk deliveries would be made: hundreds of bottles of milk in metal crates would be hurled off the lorry and sent crashing on to the pavement. Then, at about 6am, the beer was delivered. Big, heavy barrels were also thrown down on to the pavement and rolled down the chute. The noise was deafening, but it's incredible what the brain gets used to and I learned to sleep through most of it.

The most romantic sound was that of the boats on the Thames and occasionally Big Ben – we could hear the chimes depending on which way the wind was blowing, even though we lived about a mile away. As if that wasn't enough, there was noise from the tailors next door. From 7am sharp the whir of the sewing machines could be heard through the wall, and when that stopped you could hear the resident mice scurrying and scratching around. I don't remember being kept awake in all my years on Riding House Street, although if I happened to wake up I'd almost never get back to sleep again.

On Sunday mornings, when everywhere else was quiet, we would get the Salvation Army marching through, making enough noise to wake the dead. They would stop beneath our house and break into song, usually *Onward, Christian Soldiers*, and then make some speeches. After collecting a few meagre coins from people willing to give, they would march off towards Oxford Street. My capacity to operate within a sound bubble developed thus. I had the ability to shut out noise from a very early age – it's probably why I found it easy to work in clamorous newsrooms.

The top of our block was traversed by Great Titchfield Street. This was a vibrant street and still is, never boring to walk down. So many Cypriots lived there. As well as my friend Sooty and her parents, there was Vera, who lived downstairs at no. 112 with her husband, Loizis, their daughter, Nina, who had hair like Cher, and their son, Savvas. Down the road was Koulla, with her husband, Kyriacos, and their children, Maria, Sotira and George. Koulla was one of the last surviving Cypriots of the West End: she later moved into the Holcroft Court block of flats on Carburton Street and died in 2016, aged 83.

When I was small there were two greengrocer stalls on Great Titchfield Street, christened by Mum with Cypriot nicknames: the kopellia (young lads) and the yerouthkia (old lads). We never knew their real names, but we were often sent to buy potatoes from the "young lads" and onions from the "old lads". Our big grocery shop was done by Mum on Saturday mornings on Berwick Street, after she had visited the butchers on Goodge Street. Like a lot of wise shoppers, she wanted to smell and feel the produce before buying it –

but this came at a price. Her bags were always too heavy and her tired body could barely manage the walk home. Jo and I would sometimes help, but only Mum knew which stall had the best oranges and which the best tomatoes, so we usually let her get on with it.

Just up the road on Great Titchfield Street was a wet fishmongers. The whole thing was a work of art, covered floor to ceiling with the most beautiful tiles – it was an incredible shop and should never have been "modernised". Over the road was Mrs Spence, who sold sweets and the best ice cream – it came in little round cakes that you had to unwrap and put into a cone. Pepperell's the greengrocer, whose ghostly sign you can still see, was known to us as "i jinjez" (the Gingers) as the people who ran it had red hair! And on Foley Street was a small shop called Marks, run by a Jewish man of the same name. He sold the best crisps in the entire world, or so I thought at the time. These were Smiths crisps, with the little blue bag of salt, but they had been crushed into tiny, tiny pieces. They were really oily and, to my young taste buds, delicious.

About five minutes' walk away was the beautiful Fitzroy Square, the only London square designed by the architect Robert Adam. It's now home to the film director, Guy Ritchie, and to the comedian and broadcaster Griff Rhys Jones. Sometimes we would walk through to get to Warren Street or Tottenham Court Road, and in later years I was registered as a patient at the NHS surgery there. I didn't realise it at the time, but Virginia Woolf once lived there, as did George Bernard Shaw – the area was a magnet for writers, artists and bohemians.

Our neighbours were mostly European: French, Italian and Cypriot, both Greek and Turkish, with a lot of Jewish families as well. Left to themselves, Cypriots of both ethnic backgrounds coexist happily – today you can see both nationalities living and working together in areas like Haringey in North London. It was great growing up in such a colourful and, on the whole, friendly neighbourhood. Today we would call it "diverse", a big melting pot, but at the time I never gave it much thought. Yet racism did exist in parts of London. "No blacks, no dogs, no Irish" was a sign you saw in some areas in the 50s and 60s, especially in West London, where many people had arrived from the Caribbean. Mum remembered being called a "bloody foreigner" when she first arrived in the UK. Never one to take an insult lying down, she responded that they should get out of her country first and then she'd get out of theirs. She had a point, as Cyprus was still a British colony and the main reason my parents were here was because they were being taxed out of existence by the British government.

That's not to say they didn't enjoy living in London and appreciate everything the city offered. They did, after all, live a stone's throw from the best park and the best shops, John Lewis being one of them. It was Mum's favourite and she could often be spotted admiring the glassware in the basement. She was quietly pleased that she wasn't still living in her birth village, where the stifling traditions and the intense sun could have turned her into a shrivelled old crone by the age of 40.

The most colourful local of all was a tall black man known as Prince Monolulu, who would stride around in his multicoloured silk pantaloons and headdress made from ostrich feathers. I confess that, as a six-year-old, I was quite scared of him. To me, he looked like a giant, unlike anyone else on the planet. The Prince lived in nearby Maple Street and was known as a horse-racing tipster. He was a character, to say the least, and could often be heard shouting "I gotta horse, I gotta horse!"

At no. 53 lived our Armenian neighbour, Madame Julia (never referred to simply as Julia). Madame Julia would visit us in our basement, where she smoked her untipped cigarettes like a chimney and entertained us with wild stories of her life, delivered in her French accent. She had lived in Russia as a young girl and claimed she had been kidnapped one night by a man as he rode by on his horse. That man later became her husband. This story seemed somewhat far-fetched and we dismissed it as the ramblings of a lonely old woman. We couldn't imagine anyone fancying Madame Julia, with her fuzzy white hair and nicotine-stained fingernails, let alone kidnapping her. But one day I visited her flat and she showed me some of her photos. One was of a very beautiful ballerina who, it turned out, was Madame Julia aged 17. She showed me more photos and it dawned on me that she had probably been telling us the truth. You really shouldn't ever judge a book by its cover.

A lovely Italian family lived on the first floor of no. 53. I went to school with their two boys, Roberto and Ricardo, until Ricardo contracted polio and became confined to a wheelchair. The family's living arrangements became difficult, especially having to negotiate so many stairs, and eventually they were forced to move. I never saw them again, but one night, years later and out of the blue, I dreamed of Ricardo. A few days on, I was chatting to Mum in the kitchen when she broke the news: "Oh, I haven't told you. I bumped into so-and-so yesterday and, remember that Italian family next door? Well, Ricardo died a couple of days ago."

Our dearest neighbour was also the closest: Andriani, aka Kanou, who lived at no. 55 with her cat, Blackie, in two immaculate rooms on the second floor. She had a gramophone, and Jo and I would sometimes go round there for tea and to listen to her Greek music. In her collection was a copy of Edmundo Ros's *Wedding Samba*, which we thought very modern and danced to in her kitchen. Kanou was from the same village as my parents. She had a wicked sense of humour that invariably had us falling about laughing, but behind it was bitterness and tears. Under pressure from her family, Kanou had been forced to marry a man she didn't love. More to the point, her family knew that he was terminally ill. He died about a year after they were married, and such was her stubbornness and belief in fate that she never remarried. She would take me to the cemetery in Hendon where he was buried, saying she got spooked going on her own and I would be company for her, even though I was still very young. She never forgot an anniversary and would always take a bouquet of flowers to lay on his grave.

The shop that was Pepperell's the grocer on Great Titchfield Street (present day)

CELEBRATIONS

Christmas, Easter and New Year were big family get-togethers. Before he moved back to Cyprus after developing pneumonia and asthma, Mum's brother, Uncle Michael, lived up the road in Charlotte Street with his wife, Aunty Kyriacou, and their two boys, Ktori and Savva. Around the corner in Great Titchfield Street lived cousin Simos, his wife, Maria, and their daughter, my friend Sooty. Her real name is Sotira, but she was nicknamed Sooty by us and the nickname stuck. There are now countless other Cypriot Sootys all over London, both male and female, all probably because of Jo and me. We also had family living in Maple Street, Goodge Street, Wells Street and Soho. In fact, all over the West End. It felt like we owned the place.

Christmas dinner was mostly traditionally English: roast turkey and roast potatoes, along with dolmades (stuffed vine leaves) and keftedes (meatballs). After drinking bottles of whisky and Commandaria, Dad would bring out his wind-up gramophone. He loved music and this was his thing. We had stacks of 78s, most of them old Greek songs telling tales of woe: forced migration, sailors drowned at sea, lost loves. We would all sing along, my parents probably lost in memories of their homeland and the family they had left behind, and Jo and I would stay up late, either falling asleep at the table, like most Greek kids do, or going into the bedroom to play. When we were teenagers and life with Mum and Dad had become boring, we would hunker down and talk about boys and the Beatles and the Rolling Stones.

New Year's Eve was not as formal as Easter or Christmas. In Riding House Street, this meant we all sat around the big table in the kitchen rather than eating upstairs. People would drop in at random and, before 1966, when the TV came into our lives, we would listen to the chimes of Big Ben on the radio, counting down to midnight. Being in the restaurant business, Dad was usually still at work, but his arrival in the early hours meant party hats, masks and poppers. This was especially so when he worked at the 21 Club in Mayfair – they had the best party paraphernalia and quite a lot of it ended up in our house.

Mum couldn't let a saint's day slip by and 1 January was St Basil's Day (Aghios Vasilis). This was Mum's own name day, and she would prepare a tray and leave it as an offering upstairs in her bedroom. On the tray would be a plate of xerotiana, also called loukoumades (honey balls), which she had cooked earlier. Alongside this was her purse, which she believed would be blessed and full of money in the year to come, as well as a candle lit for her saint and her God.

We never did run out of money, as far as I know. We were never wealthy, but our family always seemed to have an abundance of tailored clothes, good food and holidays. My parents were very generous with their relatives, always giving gifts on special occasions. And, believe me, the years were packed with "special occasions" – countless birthdays, engagements, weddings and christenings. You never visited someone's house without taking them something, even if it was just a packet of biscuits. Mum would always say she couldn't turn up with "sherka themena" (hands tied up) or words to that effect.

I don't know how they managed financially. As a chef, Dad made no more than £20-30 a week, and Mum earned half that. Dad would hand over his pay packet every Friday, keeping £3 to cover the tobacco for his pipe, his daily cup of tea at the Glory during afternoon break and his newspaper, back then the *Daily Telegraph*. From this meagre income they clothed us, fed us and kept us warm and happy. When I think of the benefits available now, I wonder how people like my parents managed on zero handouts. Nevertheless, they did, and this was down to the selflessness of Dad and the good management of Mum, the villager who left school at nine years old and who loved and cared for her family with the fierceness of a lioness.

Christmas in our sitting room. From left: Sooty, Mum, me, Mariou and Simos (Sooty's parents) and Dad, 1965

Simos with balloon and Dad, enjoying a drop of the hard stuff around the Christmas table

Me with Mum, Xmas 1965

Dad (right) and his fellow chefs at the 21 Room Club, Curzon Street, Mayfair

LIQUID GOLD

Olive oil. That stuff that looks like liquid gold and is an everyday essential in a Greek family's life. My parents' taste in food barely changed during their years in London – hardly surprising, because when they first came over the food, according to Mum, was mostly boiled meat and foul-smelling cabbage. She always joked that it was the foreigners who taught the English how to eat, and I reckon she had a point. As a family, we ate everything our relatives in Cyprus ate. Once or twice a week we had legumes such as black-eyed beans with spinach, or chard dressed with olive oil and lemon with a side dish of sardines, or bean stew with tomatoes, carrots and celery. We also ate huge amounts of meat – now that I'm virtually a veggie, I'm embarrassed to admit it.

As if she didn't work hard enough, Mum regularly made dolmades and keftedes, both extremely time-consuming. Anyone who tasted hers said they were the best they had ever eaten. She also used to make her own yoghurt, with a "pikardi" (culture) given to her by relatives at the Glory. This was fascinating to witness. The yoghurt would be poured into glasses and then placed snugly around a boiled kettle, covered with a blanket and left to set overnight. It was the closest thing to real Cypriot yoghurt.

Years later I discovered Tims Greek-style yoghurt, currently sold in supermarkets here in the UK. It's delicious and tastes just like Mum's Cypriot yoghurt. I happened to mention this to Jason, another London-born Greek Cypriot who works at my hairdressers in London, Inanch, and he told me that his uncles run the business. If that wasn't coincidence enough, their early workshop, founded by Euripides Nicolaou in 1949, was initially on Warren Street and then moved to, you guessed it, Riding House Street. They may have even known my parents, but alas there's no one alive today who can tell us. The name Tims, by the way, comes from Michael Timotheou, Jason's grandfather, who joined his brother-in-law Euripides in the business. It was then passed down to the four uncles who run it today.

A lot of Greek food is cooked in a big pot or slowly roasted in a large tin. The recipes are really very simple: afelia (pork cooked in wine with coriander seeds), tava (lamb with cumin), stifado (beef cooked with onions). One of my favourite vegetables is bamia, also known as ladies' fingers, okra or bhindi. Bamia cooked in tomatoes and onions over sliced potatoes – and served with a glug of olive oil, of course – is just delicious.

Once or twice a year, my parents would receive a consignment of food shipped directly from relatives in Cyprus, most of it produced on our own land. Dad would go over to the food importers Katsouris Brothers in North London and come back with a large wooden crate. We were never sure exactly what our relatives had packed and the anticipation was part of the fun. There would be fresh oranges, halloumi, preserved pork packed in tins of lard (basta), honey, poxamadthia (crispy breads with sesame) and green olives picked from our very own trees. There would be tins of olive oil, too, smooth and dark. So good was the oil that Mum found herself selling it to neighbours who came round pleading for a bottle. She charged five shillings (about 25p) for 75cl, which was probably quite a lot of money then.

The olive must be one of nature's finest gifts. I was in Cyprus in 1969 during picking season and couldn't resist going out with the family to harvest olives from our ancient, gnarled trees. Because of Akanthou's location, on the coast in the foothills of the mountains, most of the fields spread out towards the sea. It was a gloriously hot day and the horizon was shimmering; the water was as still as glass and as blue as ink. I jumped off the tractor and headed down with Dad and the rest of the family. Sheets were spread out to collect the olives and work began – this particular field must have had at least 20 trees, so it was going to be a long day. As a London kid, brought up in a small flat, this was bliss. I loved the freedom of being in the middle of nowhere, of breathing in the stillness, of hearing no sound. I left the others to carry on and sat down to read my book, my back resting against the trunk of an old friend. Gazing out towards the sea, knowing my feet were placed where my grandparents' feet had once been, I drifted away into the sweetest of sleeps. Years later, I can still recall the complete contentment I felt on that day.

Cousin Ktori's olive trees at Tsappi, Akanthou, 2010 (under occupation when photo taken)

Cousin Ktori with his olives, 2010

Picking carobs in Akanthou, Dad is on the right, 1969

CHIEF MOUSER

Another unforgettable character was Ginger, the cat from Birmingham. He was beautiful, with the most distinctive markings and golden eyes. Ginger originally belonged to my cousin Andrew, but he and his wife had been about to sell their fish and chip shop in Birmingham and, to my horror, leave the cat behind. I'd been staying with them for a few days and the plan was for them to drive me back to Riding House Street on their day off. I had fallen for Ginger and there was no way I was going to leave him behind.

So, Ginger came to London. Mum was not pleased, to put it mildly. We had kept cats previously, but they had either died or gone missing and Mum was glad to have one less thing to think about. When I turned up with Ginger she threw a fit. I was expecting it, but the poor cat cowered under the kitchen table, hoping never to come out. After her protestations died down he eventually emerged, and I was determined he would stay. Over the days and weeks that followed, Ginger became part of the family, beguiling us with his cleverness and beauty.

He had his own chair by the electric fire in the kitchen. If a visitor sat on it he would stare them out, and if they happened to get up momentarily he would take their place in a flash. He was full of tricks and would often rattle the kitchen doorknob from outside and actually let himself in. The basement and kitchen were his domain and he slept in the junk room next door. He wasn't allowed upstairs into the bedrooms, but I'd occasionally sneak him into my room where he would sleep the sleep of kings – until Mum threw him out.

She did grow to love him, but she also had little patience for his naughtiness and often ticked him off. One day, holding a cat grudge, he lay in wait for her at the bottom of the stairs, leaping out and nipping her ankle as she walked by. Everyone thought it was hilarious, as did she eventually, and I think he went up a few notches in her estimation after that.

Ginger had a job, chief mouser, and he was very good at it. There were mice everywhere. You could hear their scratching through the walls and occasionally they were foolish enough to venture out. Once, a mouse came running into the kitchen while I was doing my homework. I screamed and jumped on the chair, and Dad got really annoyed and started shouting. That made it even worse: the more he shouted the more I screamed, and finally I burst into tears. This ridiculous scene carried on until the mouse was caught and dispatched to mouse heaven. Calmness returned, but I was miffed by Dad's attitude and left to wonder why men don't understand women. But, together, Dad and Ginger were the A-team. They pounced when they had to, earning them many brownie points. Ginger became part of our family, but most of all he became Dad's cat.

When Dad came home for his afternoon break, Ginger would stretch out along his body as he reclined on a chair.

The cat's diet consisted of raw steak that Dad brought home from whichever restaurant he was working at. Ginger was strong and lean and very sharp, but he was also a bit of a softie. At night he would wait on the corner of Riding House and Wells streets for Dad to come home from work, no matter how late it was, and the two of them would walk up to the house together like old friends. Who says cats aren't loyal? Or was it the smell of steak in Dad's pocket that kept him interested? I like to think not.

Ginger chancing Mum's wrath by sitting on our "best" armchair

Ginger with my cousins Chris and his sister Angela in our basement kitchen

FLYING THE FLAG

I was aware during the 50s that a campaign was under way for the union of Cyprus with Greece, fought for by a guerrilla movement called EOKA. Cyprus was a British colony, but the natives were becoming restless. There were tales of torture and hangings by British soldiers and there was a lot of resentment towards the British masters, especially among the youth of the island.

As the child of Cypriot parents, I heard whisperings that became embedded in my imagination. They talked quietly about men being hidden in basements, about leaflets being distributed. About someone they knew being chased across the fields and shot dead. About a man from Akanthou called Zitti who was a traitor, the worst of all crimes. Someone we knew was writing patriotic slogans under kitchen chairs in London, and we thought it was funny when their English friends visited and sat on them.

All this disturbed me somewhat, but I reckoned it was happening far away and wouldn't affect our safe family life in London. To some extent that was true, but we weren't untouched by events. I remember endless boring Sundays at political conferences listening to speeches given by the Cypriot "elite". I used to wonder why they all shouted so much. Forced to sit through those patriotic lectures we could barely understand, Jo and I wished we'd been born anything other than Cypriot.

We would also be made to accompany Dad on marches to Trafalgar Square and Downing Street, where speeches would be made and petitions handed in. This was marginally more exciting. Then there were visits to the offices of the Adelphotita, the Greek Cypriot Brotherhood, on Fitzroy Square. We were regularly made to go along to hear the latest on what was happening "back home". One occasion was different to the rest: when the Cypriot leader, Archbishop Makarios, came to the Adelphotita on his first public appearance since his return from British exile in the Seychelles (could have been worse!). The atmosphere was electric and I really did feel something special was happening.

Even though we were born in London, our parents made sure we spoke Greek before we spoke English. But being able to speak Greek wasn't enough. We were expected to read and write it, too. Jo, 10 years older than me, was a fantastic first teacher and I remember her sitting me down at home and going through the basics. Yet getting to the next stage meant hard work and long hours, when all we wanted was to be outside playing with our friends and having fun.

After primary school finished for the day, I stayed behind twice a week to attend Greek school. A Greek teacher was hired and the Cypriot kids (about 30 of us) would gather in the school hall to spend the next hour or so learning to read, write and polish our grammar. And also to sing. Our music teacher, Pieris Zarmas, was a Cypriot gifted with a booming baritone voice and great enthusiasm. He also played the piano, duetting with our teacher, Miss Nikoli, while we giggled because we thought they fancied each other. What we weren't to know was that Zarmas would go on to become a hugely respected opera singer. Originally from Akanthou, the same small village as my parents, he had come to London to study music at the academies and taught us in his free time. He went on to fame and fortune, singing on the stages of Milan, Barcelona and Athens, and captivating audiences at the Opera House in Bonn over a period of some 40 years.

Things were different for my sister, whose learning of the Greek language wasn't as straightforward as mine. Jo would sometimes turn up to school with bags under her eyes and her English teacher, Mrs Thorpe, became suspicious. This was back in the late 40s when Jo was aged seven or eight, admittedly too young to be so knackered. "Why are you looking so tired, child?" Mrs Thorpe demanded. "I don't know, Miss, maybe it's because I'm doing Greek classes after school," Jo replied. I don't know if it was school policy back then, or if Mrs Thorpe was a forerunner of the BNP, but she didn't like it one bit. My parents were called in and told to put a stop to it: "Joanna was born in this country so she's English, and English should be her first language. She can always learn Greek later on," they were told. So that was that. No more Greek school for Jo, although those words forever riled my mother and would exclaim that it wasn't an Englishman who'd spawned her daughter. It's to my sister's credit that she went on to speak five languages.

The pinnacles of our Greek education were the celebrations

to commemorate national days, like the one on 28 October. This is Ohi Day (No Day), when Greece's prime minister, Ioannis Metaxas, turned down Mussolini's request to allow Italian troops into Greece during World War II. Somehow, us little Londoners were turned into Greek folk heroes and heroines, and the brightest of the class were chosen to recite pieces by poets such as Kostis Palamas. There onstage, dressed in national costume, we would deliver our lines and hold the Greek national flag aloft. We could see our mums and dads in the audience brimming with pride, huge smiles on their faces – they had done their job for their motherland! Their children may have been born in a faraway land, but they had Greek blood in their veins. For us, though, walking down the street in those costumes was excruciatingly embarrassing – I dreaded bumping into my English friends as they would have made fun of me mercilessly. I so resented those classes at the time, but without them I'd now be staring in frustration at the Greek alphabet, not having a clue what any of it meant.

Cypriot national costume: Sooty, Nikki, me, Nina

Greek class at All Souls Primary School. Me (far left), Sooty (fourth from right), then cousins Savva and Ktori. Panos is at the end of the first row, with Nina and Helen behind him

Pieris Zarmas, our music teacher, after he became a famous opera singer

KIDS IN THE CITY

At my primary school, All Souls, there were a lot of children belonging to migrant parents. The West End was a real mix and mostly we all got on well without ever questioning nationality or race, but this was the 50s and there was some racism. Once, I was in the playground when I saw one of my friends crying. I went up and asked her what the matter was, and she said someone had laughed at her because she was black. I felt sorry that she was crying, but I was too young to understand her problem – it had never occurred to me that she was different to anyone else. I went home and told Mum, whose response was typical. She assured me that we were all the same underneath, no matter what colour we were on top. I've never forgotten her words and often think about that little girl and wonder what she's doing today.

I remember a lot of playtime at All Souls. Skipping was big back then, as was the hula hoop, which had us girls whirling like dervishes all over the playground. Then there was hopscotch, a game that goes back centuries but was still hugely popular with boys and girls. Being a tomboy, I also liked to play "fag cards" with the boys. We placed little illustrated cards found in cigarette packets up against the wall and flicked a coin at them to see if we could knock them down.

Before All Souls I went to a nursery school on Great Windmill Street in Soho. I was about three when I first joined St James's and St Paul's, now called Soho Parish Primary School. Every morning I'd hold on to Mum's hand for the walk to school, which for a small child must have seemed like miles, even though it was just 10 minutes for a grown-up. Was the walk scary? After all, this was seedy old Soho where "bad things" could happen to you. The sex shops, the doorways offering exotic call girls, the red lights glowing in the windows – it was all there. But I was completely unaware of this, being just three years old. What I remember most is the bustle of the market stalls on Berwick Street and the black and white cat we would stop to stroke. To me, Soho was colourful and enchanting, full of life and markets and cats.

A few years later, in 1958, Paul Raymond opened his Revuebar in Walker's Court, a lane off Berwick Street full of grungy sex shops and garish neon. It was here that punters in London could see full-frontal nudity for the very first time. But, for me, the most fascinating attraction was the fountain in the foyer that changed colour every few seconds, from neon green to blue, orange and red. This transfixed me every time I walked by and continued to do so well into my teens. Alas, as I write, Walker's Court is being redeveloped – the further sanitisation of Soho in the name of gentrification.

Going outside to play was one of the greatest joys of my childhood. Back then, our streets were quiet and safe and virtually devoid of cars. Even today, the back streets of the

West End are quiet in the evenings and at weekends, with most of the office workers miraculously disappearing and leaving the place to the few residents lucky enough to live there.

I was a very keen roller skater. I first learned the art on a pair of archaic skates that belonged to my sister. They were rather medieval-looking contraptions: there was a key that turned two little metal clips over the toes to secure the skate over the foot. I would put them on and move slowly over the basement lino until I found my feet, and later I graduated to proper skates and the street pavement. In the end, the more uneven the pavement the better I liked it – skating was more exciting when the surface wasn't smooth. There were skating races: two of us would agree to race around the block, skating away from a central point and in opposite directions. We would pass each other somewhere in the middle before reaching the finish line, approaching it from different ends of the street. It was pure city adrenaline.

On one occasion, while playing outside, my friends and I came close to catastrophe. It was 5 November, fireworks night. A group of us had gathered outside our house with bangers, Catherine wheels, rockets and squibs and we started setting them off. Soon a policeman made his way towards us: "You're not allowed to play with these in the street, it's too dangerous," he said. "But, officer, we don't have a garden, only a backyard," we replied. It was no use, he wouldn't have it, so we went next door to no. 55, which had a yard almost twice the size of ours at no. 57.

All was going well until one of the squibs took off from the wall where it was pinned and headed straight for Matthew.

Matthew's hand shot up over his eye and he began running around, screaming. We all froze. Had he lost his eye? Was he blinded? Why had that stupid policeman told us to move on? My sister, being the oldest and bravest, carefully prised Matthew's hand away. His eye was covered in black soot and we had no idea if there was any permanent damage. We ran with Matthew to the A&E at the Middlesex and it turned out he had been incredibly lucky: the squib had hit him just above the eye and the only thing he had lost was his eyebrow. We were petrified about telling his mum and when we did, she fainted. So much for the streets being dangerous.

Another time, Sooty somehow impaled her arm on the railings at our primary school. There was blood everywhere and the teachers were called. Some brave person was dispatched to tell Sooty's mum – the reaction was hysterics. Full of trepidation, Sooty's mum went to the hospital where she heard her daughter's screams coming from behind a curtain. Ashen-faced, she was staggering along the corridor when a hospital cleaner took pity on her and offered her a cigarette. She was horrified. She was a good Cypriot woman who had never held a cigarette in her hand, let alone smoked one – only "good-time girls" did that! We used to think the impaling story incredibly funny: Sooty's mum lived in constant fear for her daughter's life and any slight mishap would send her into a tailspin. Luckily, Sooty survived the impaling and all that's left today is a juicy scar on the inside of her right arm.

None of us kids were angels and none of us came through unscarred. We were always falling over or trying it on. I remember putting my head through the railings outside

Sooty's house, just to see better into their basement, and then not being able to pull it back, my ears blocking a clean withdrawal. I must have looked very silly and I was too embarrassed to call for help. Eventually I managed to extricate my head, to my great and everlasting relief.

Around our house were a lot of bomb sites, and Foley Street and Maple Street had mountains of rubble. They were, I suppose, the adventure parks of the day, beloved by boys like Mick Stavri and Matthew, who both lived on Maple Street. They were the funniest and brightest of boys, always laughing, playing pranks and telling jokes.

Their friends were just as bad. Take Kenny Harte, a notorious prankster who over the years had picked up some choice Cypriot Greek words from them and some bad habits. One day, an insurance man came knocking on Matthew's door asking for a Mr Villoz Mattheou (Mr Penis Mattheou). Kenny had secretly filled in a newspaper advert for a life insurance quote for this Villoz Mattheou. Matthew's dad, who answered the door, started laughing: "E yeneka, ela n'akousis!" (Hey, wife, come and listen to this!). He made the insurance man repeat that he wanted to speak to Mr Villoz Mattheou and, believe it or not, the man with zero awareness of what he was saying, made a sale.

With Mick, his humour and brashness came from his mum, Elenara, who together with Mick's dad ran the grocers on Cleveland Street. During a bread strike one year, she could be heard yelling down the phone to Wonderloaf: "Where's my fucki' bre'? My customas wan their fucki' bre'!" I wouldn't be surprised if they made a special delivery the next day just for her. Mick's dad, Andreas, was quieter than his wife but nevertheless a character. Matthew remembers him chasing a Pakistani man down Cleveland Street and throwing a potato at him, after the man asked to buy just one potato – anathema to Greeks, who usually purchase their food by the cartload.

Years later, Mick told me an extraordinary story. He and his friend Jack Georgiou were coming home in the early hours of the morning after a night on the lash. They had dropped Jack's girlfriend off at home and were making their way to Mick's house on Maple Street, where Jack was to crash for the night. Dying for a pee, they decided to urinate through the nearest letterbox. Just as they were thinking this, the GPO Tower loomed into view, so up the steps they went and into the letterbox they did pee. With job done, they walked the 50 yards across the road to Mick's house and let themselves in. Within seconds a violent explosion ripped through the air, rocking the house and half the street. Shards of glass and metal fell to the ground from the tower. "Bloody hell, what have we done? That wasn't us, was it?" thought Mick in complete panic. No, Mick, it wasn't you. It was the IRA and you were very lucky to be alive.

School holidays could have been a nightmare, what with both my parents working and no one to look after us. It wasn't so much of a problem when I was at grammar school, as Jo was still at college and could keep an eye on me, but primary school was different. Our extended family became our knight in shining armour. Mariou, Sooty's mum, was married to my second cousin Simo on Dad's side, which meant she was very close to us. Well, to Greeks, second cousin means close. Mariou was like my second mum and I spent all my primary school holidays at Sooty's. We generally got on very well and would play all day, but even the best of friends could sometimes fall out, especially when cooped up in two small rooms. There were some huge spats that ended with Mariou's nerves frayed and her "two daughters" wildly indignant and in tears.

To give everyone breathing space we were often taken to Regent's Park. Mariou, who worked from home in tailoring, would take her day's work of jackets and sit on the grass while Sooty and I played until supper time. Our favourite pastime was the swings in the playground: we would swing for hours and have a go on the roundabout when we'd had enough. We occasionally played football or, if there were enough of us, rounders. I remember once pushing my toy pram to the park. Wrapped up in it was a dismembered leg from one of my dolls, which we used to play cricket. Needs must.

When I was older, I would go with Jo to visit family friends in Notting Hill during the school holidays. We were very close to the various strands of the Avgousti family and most of them lived in a tall stucco house on Colville Road, a stone's throw from Portobello. There was Andreas and his sisters, plus their assorted children. One of the sisters, Avgoustou, had been at primary school with Mum in Akanthou: they would still shriek with laughter whenever they got together and their close friendship was passed down the generations. Jo and I were very friendly with Avgoustou's daughters, Helen and Thalia. I'm now godmother to Thalia's first son, Jason, and we put our shared taste in music down to when I "blew" on him as a baby, part of the rite observed during an Orthodox christening to ensure the baby takes after the godparent. I'm not sure if I blew hard enough on my goddaughter Helen, but perhaps I did as she now lives in Cyprus! As for my little English goddaughter, Mia, she's Roman Catholic so I didn't have to blow on her at all.

My other best friend at the time was Andrew. He was part of the Avgousti family and his father owned a restaurant on the King's Road. Andrew was around my age and his brother, my godbrother Douglas, was a few years younger than Jo. We spent a lot of time together, usually playing games in the large basement of their home on St Leonard's Terrace in Chelsea, which backed on to Sir Laurence Olivier's house. He, incidentally, once told Andrew to shut up for making too much noise playing football in the garden. Fancy being told by Sir Larry to shut up! It's Andrew's claim to fame.

One of our favourite games was Cock of Cock Castle, devised by Douglas and his cousins Helen and Nick. It was essentially hide and seek in the dark, and was very scary. Someone would leap out and announce he was Cock of Cock Castle, then chase everyone else around – usually it was Douglas who took on this role and I remember being frightened half to death. It was all good, bloodcurdling fun and we'd scream with laughter afterwards.

As a postscript to the Olivier incident, more than 25 years later, Andrew, a budding architect, was involved in developing the design for Olivier's dressing room at the National Theatre. Funny how the world turns.

Like all good things, playtime had to come to an end and by 8pm I was usually in bed. Ours wasn't a cosy house and

I would baulk at being sent all alone to a cold room on the first floor while down in the basement kitchen was warmth and laughter. Mum had a habit of lighting a night candle beside an icon of the Virgin Mary, just next to my bed. The candle would throw shadows across the walls while the icon, depending on the way you looked at it, would morph into an image of St George killing the dragon. This was terrifying for a child who, like me, had an overactive imagination. I would lie in bed with eyes tightly shut, convinced that if I opened them I would see a ghost peering down at me.

When Jo eventually came to bed I'd breathe a sigh of relief and feel safe again. She would either read or listen to the radio while doing her homework, and I would usually find myself awake and listening, too. Radio Luxembourg was big back then. This was around the time Elvis exploded on to the scene – we'd never heard anything like him before and Jo became Elvis-crazy, playing *Heartbreak Hotel* over and over again. When rockers like Chuck Berry, Jerry Lee Lewis and Little Richard came along, that's when music really became interesting. It wasn't long before Radio Caroline and pirate radio came into our lives and then we really did stay up all night.

During these nights, Jo's radio started broadcasting a real-time nightmare. It was the early 60s and the world was being brought to the brink of nuclear war. We were in the middle of the Cuban missile crisis, a standoff between the US and the Soviet Union over the installation of nuclear missiles on Cuba. Jo was glued to her radio night after night – her fear became my fear, and for a 12-year-old who didn't fully understand what was going on, that was huge. I remember that fear more than anything else and the thought of us all dying: Mum, Dad, the cat. Thankfully, the 13-day crisis was averted and the most dangerous period in the history of the world was over. Jo and I could go back to listening to our music and singing along to our favourite songs.

Reading my book at nursery school in Soho

Some of our class at All Souls primary

Gloria, the May Queen, at All Souls primary

Dancing the maypole at primary school

Regent's Park circa 1950. Left to right: Angelou (Matthew's mum), Nouna Georgia, Sotiris (Matthew's dad), my dad, Uncle Soto, Matthew aged about two, Tata Elias

Regent's Park circa 1950s. Jo, Helen and Thalia are standing, with Stavros, me and Matthew at the front

George, me and Eleni on the 'Japanese' bridge in Regent's Park

Sooty and me, Regent's Park

FAMILY RESTAURANTS

Most of my aunts and uncles ran a restaurant of some sort. Two stood out above all the others: the Unity on the King's Road and the Globe on Richmond Hill, old-fashioned places with silver service, white damask table linen and very polite staff. The Unity was owned by Uncle Avgousti and Aunty Maria, the parents of Andrew and Douglas. Uncle Avgousti was always impeccably dressed and very courteous. The Unity served high-end English and Continental cuisine with a couple of traditional Greek dishes thrown in, like moussaka and shish kebabs. Years later, after they sold the restaurant, Aunty Maria gave me a plate from the restaurant as a memento. This white dish, trimmed with a band of maroon and gold, is still with me and I treasure it.

The Globe was of the same standard and owned by Uncle George and Aunty Vass, Dad's first cousin. What I remember most about the Globe was its location. Perched high on the road in Richmond, it had a terrace at the back overlooking the Thames where we would eat on warm summer evenings. Beyond the terrace was a small golf course, its banks of green rolling down to the river and across to Richmond Bridge.

I have blissful memories of these two restaurants and they weaved magic in my young mind's eye.

I've always been impressed by how these families from remote villages in Cyprus ended up owning two of London's classiest restaurants, and in the most exclusive parts of town. Call it luck or a sixth sense, who knows, but the fact is they did and they made a wonderful job of it.

There were others, too, including the Forum on the Fulham Road. This was owned by Uncle Polivi and Aunty Braxou. When he wasn't doing the cooking, Uncle Polivi would sit in the restaurant's basement kitchen studying horse-racing form or doing the pools. He loved the thrill of gambling and I'm sure the local betting office went into mourning the day he died. Uncle Polivi and Aunty Braxou lived in the flat upstairs with their only son, Nick, who when he was older was branded the black sheep of the family because he was a rebel and wore a sheepskin gilet.

Then there was the Half Moon cafe on Fulham Palace Road, owned by mum's very dear Godson, George Ktori, together with his wife Savvou. They offered good quality food and the place was always busy. George and Savvou worked hard, getting up in the small hours to go to market and coming back to serve the best breakfast and lunch in the area. We'd be invited on a Sunday, their only day off, to eat roast lamb with them. George would always insist on driving us back home, however late it was. They loved and respected my parents very much and would have done anything for them.

Another restaurant that played a significant part in our lives was the Flamingo in South Norwood, owned by my godfather

Tata Taki and godmother Nouna Maria. It originally belonged to Nouna Maria's father, but my Godparents inherited the place when he died. The Flamingo was an absolute hoot. We spent many happy hours there, always in hysterics, because that family is one of the funniest I've had the privilege to spend time with. They also had a rather large tabby cat affectionately known as Seymeni, a Turkish name bestowed on him by my Godfather who thought he was beautiful, but also a little shrewd. It would take us ages to get to South Norwood from the West End. One of them would always have to drive us back home after closing time, and closing time could be anything between midnight and 3am – whenever the punters had had their fill. It got so late one night that one of Tata Taki and Nouna Maria's children, Johnny, decided to show the stragglers enough was enough. He went upstairs, put on his pyjamas and came back down. He didn't say a word, but sat staring at them with a silly look on his face. When they eventually twigged they saw the funny side and left, laughing all the way home. I guess that's why that family and that restaurant were so loved.

The Hope Dining Rooms, at 111 Holloway Road, was owned by Dad's relatives Katina and Adamos, while the Grove Restaurant at no. 249 belonged to Aunty Maria and Uncle George. This was more of a working man's restaurant, but it served very good food and never seemed to close. We sometimes visited on a Sunday, when we'd be taken to a table at the far end of the premises while the family tried to be sociable and manage the restaurant at the same time. It was how a lot of Cypriots lived, running a business while trying to run a family. Sometimes, someone would lose out.

Usually it was the kids, who were left to fend for themselves and didn't get much parental help with schoolwork, but who just as surely would get a walloping if they came home with bad results.

Of course, my own parents dabbled in restaurants, but Dad had no eye for business and little interest in accumulating money. During the war years, before I came along, they owned a little cafe on Charlotte Place, just off Goodge Street, where they also had their wedding party. Dad, being the great businessman he was, bought the cafe for £30 and sold it for £20. He flogged it to a man who ran it like a Cypriot kafene, and because it was at no. 3 it was always known as To Tria. He had it for years, but in 1990 it was sold again and became known as Da Paolo. This popular little Italian restaurant remains there to this day and probably rakes in a fortune.

The Globe on Richmond Hill owned by Uncle George and Aunty Vass

Uncle Avgousti inside his Unity restaurant on the King's Road, Chelsea

Unity restaurant menu cover

LES ENTREES

Escalope de Veau Marsala	16/–
Escalope Milanaise	16/–
Escalope Holstein	16/–
Roast Chicken	14/–
Caneton Rôti Apple Sauce (Breast)	20/–
Caneton à l'Orange (Leg)	17/6
Braised Ham Sauce Madère	14/–
Prawns Pilaf	14/–
Entrecôte Bordelaise	18/6
½ Roast Pheasant	20/–
Chicken Pilaf	14/–
Mousaka	17/6
Shish Kebab à la Grecque	17/6

GRILLS

Grilled Rump Steak	18/6
Grilled Fillet Steak	20/–
Grilled Lamb Cutlets	15/–
Grilled Entrecôte	18/6
Grilled Veal Chop	17/–

COLD BUFFET

Cold Chicken and Salad	16/6
Cold Ham and Salad	14/–

WINES BY THE GLASS
(approximately ¼ bottle)

Beaujolais	5/–
Castel Danielis	5/–
Demestica Red	5/–
Demestica White	5/–
Aphrodite	5/–
Retsina	5/–

LES LEGUMES

Broccoli	3/–
Spinach	3/–
Beans	3/–
Peas	3/–
Sprouts	3/–
New Potatoes	2/–
Fried Potatoes	2/–
Sauté Potatoes	2/–

SALADS

Salades au choix Vinaigrette	4/–

SWEETS

Banana Split	5/–
Peach Melba	5/–
Coupe Jacques	5/–
Fruit Salad and Cream	5/–
Lemon or Jam Pancakes	4/–
Crème Caramel	4/–
Baklava	3/–
Halva	3/–
Turkish Delight	3/–
Omelette Confiture	6/6

ICES

Tutti Frutti	3/6
Vanilla	3/6
Chocolate	3/6
Strawberry	3/6
Coffee	3/6

Mushrooms on Toast	5/6
Cheese and Biscuits	5/–
Coffee	2/6

Unity restaurant menu

Poly's Kebab House on the Holloway Road. Dad standing to the left of Father Grigorios (now Archbishop of Thyateira and Great Britain). Next to Dad are Sotiris (Aspris), Minas and cousin Savvas

With local neighbourhood friends at Ioakimi's and Loukia's restaurant, the Cypriana on Rathbone Street, W1

Da Paolo on Charlotte Place. The restaurant was owned by my parents in the 1940's before its present incarnation

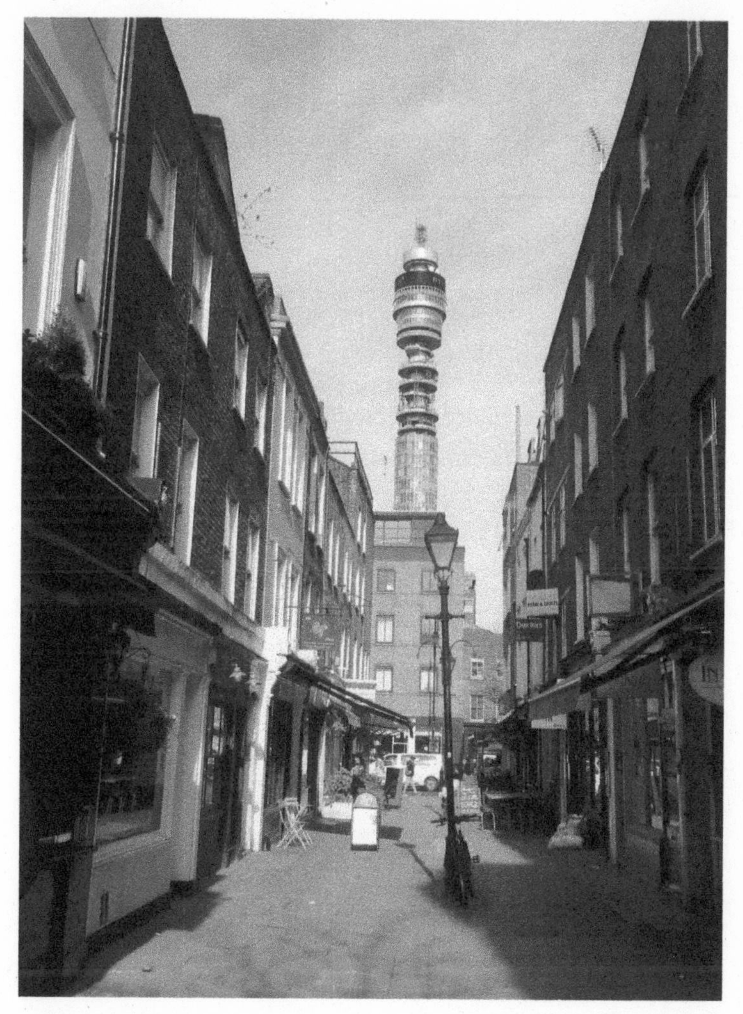

(as previous)

THE GLORY

The Glory (currently a Nando's) was the restaurant that played the biggest part in our lives. It was located on Goodge Street, a two-minute walk from Riding House Street, and in the early days every engagement, wedding and christening party in the community was held there. The Cypriots always referred to the Glory as Nikoletto's, after one of the partners who owned it. The other partner was George Ndortsi. When both partners died, the restaurant was passed down to Michael, Nikoletto's son-in-law, and Ndortsi's son Nick, who was married to my second cousin Evangelia. In our world, that meant our family ran the restaurant and we had a lot of rights there.

The restaurant was divided into two rooms. The first served English food to mainly English customers, but the room next door was for the sole use of Cypriot men. They would go there to catch up on news from back home, argue about politics and football, and read the Greek papers. The Glory was also the first port of call for the migrant villagers from Akanthou who came to London in the 40s and 50s, arriving with little but a piece of paper bearing the name and address of the restaurant. They were looking for shelter and any work that was available. An enormous amount of help was offered by their compatriots, even in those hard times, and the community flourished under the Glory's protection.

This was the commendable, charitable and squeaky-clean version of the restaurant, but the Glory also had a dark side. Deep in its bowels, down in the basement, you could often find men gambling illegally at card tables, sweating and cursing until the early hours or when their luck ran out. Hundreds if not thousands of pounds were won or lost there. The Glory could make you or break you, depending on which floor you chose to frequent.

Dad always chose to stay on the ground floor. He would drop in on his afternoon break, order a cup of tea, light up his pipe (which he named the Queen Mary after the ocean liner's vast funnels) and catch up with old friends. It was as close as he could get to being back in his village, and I'm sure it helped numb the sense of loss he must have felt every day he was away from Cyprus.

He could talk for hours and hours (and bore us kids stiff) about his homeland, reminiscing about how he worked his fields and about the sea, the mountains and his dream to return. Yet while many a dream was spun in that cafe, many were also shattered. When the Turks invaded Cyprus in July 1974, London's Greek Cypriots sat in the Glory and watched, helpless, as their lands were seized and their very raison d'être was shattered. After the invasion, the need to gather at the Glory became more urgent. Every snippet of news was exchanged, every newspaper scanned and every missing person's name checked again and again. Like all the inhabitants of Akanthou and most of the towns and villages in the north of Cyprus, these families became refugees, run out of their homes and destined not to return.

In happier times, in the early years, the Glory was where we held our celebrations. Laughter and song would fill the restaurant. The best Cypriot violinist would be brought in to play: Papou Nikoli, the head of the Avgousti family. He was an incredible musician who could make his old violin sing, creating the sweetest music in his duets with Hailos (Michael), who played the laoudo, an instrument similar to a mandolin. Of course, they played only traditional Cypriot music, but that's all the older generation wanted to hear. Even us younger ones thought it was fantastic and everyone would be up on their feet, dancing until they dropped.

With Cypriots, it is very much a free-for-all. Whoever feels the urge will get up and dance, whether they are gatecrashing someone else's moment or not. That includes the kids. I know I could never be stopped – I would run on to the dance floor regardless of who was on it. No one ever minded, and in fact they thought it proved that us London-born kids were actually Cypriot village children in disguise, with dancing in our blood.

I'm not sure if the musicians were ever formally paid, but they always went home with a lot of money in their pockets. Tradition had it that whoever was dancing would throw money (usually notes) into a tray at the feet of the musician as a mark of appreciation. It didn't stop there. If you were a friend or relative of the dancer and were moved by the vision of your loved one performing, you would put money in the plate. If an unmarried girl was dancing and you saw an unmarried guy throw money into the plate, you would know he fancied her. A lot of gossip and fantasies were spawned over things as trivial as this. By the time we went home, half the guests would have been married off and the next wedding invitations sent out.

The Glory restaurant on Goodge Street, W1

Inside the Glory: Dad, Ioakimis Sotiriou, Mihalis Paraskeva. A rare chance to relax with friends

Helping out at a Glory wedding: Yiannis Paraskeva (Pouffouros), Kostis Yiangou, Kyriacos Adamou and Dad

Another Glory wedding: Tata Takis, Uncle George Evangelou and Dad

DOWN THE AISLE

If there's one thing a Cypriot loves, it's a wedding. Everyone is invited to everyone else's, whether they're a close relative or someone you've occasionally chatted with – I've been to weddings with up to 2,000 guests. Back in the 50s, though, they were mostly held in small family restaurants with about 50 guests, and were always on a Sunday, the day most people didn't have to work. As London's Cypriots prospered, the receptions moved to large town halls such as St Pancras, Shoreditch or Hackney, or hotels such as the Kenilworth or the Marriott. Now, those with limitless wealth choose the Grosvenor on Park Lane or, classier still, the Dorchester.

My parents loved weddings, and Jo and I were always expected to turn up with them. They were mostly OK, but after we morphed into stroppy teenagers we found some of them excruciatingly boring. All the food was prepared by the family. A host of aunties and other assorted relatives would gather in our basement kitchen, rolling up their sleeves and gossiping and laughing as they made the dolmades and keftedes. Someone would have made the kourabiethes – shortbread biscuits filled with chopped nuts that were given to guests who came up to greet the happy couple at the top table. Hundreds of them would arrive at our house in boxes; we would have to wrap each one in a paper serviette and twist each end to hold it in.

The men played their part, too, but not until the big day. In the early morning they would gather at the wedding venue, where cars and vans would deliver a massive load of fresh food ordered by the parents of the couple. It was the job of the men to prepare it all. Everything had to be washed and sliced: tomatoes, cucumbers, lettuce, olives, halloumi, salami. Roast chickens had to be cut up, legs of lamb sliced. When all the prep was finished, the men would go home to change into their best clothes. Dad had some very smart handmade suits, made to measure by a godson or a cousin in Soho. He always looked dapper, but he couldn't put his feet up and enjoy the rest of the day. No, he had more "duties" to carry out.

As the favoured uncle of half of Cyprus, he often had to act as the token dad and walk female relatives, whose fathers were still in Cyprus, down the aisle. So Dad had to dash home to get ready, rush over to wherever the bride was, ride in the wedding car with her, do the aisle thing and, of course, pose for photos after the ceremony. We have many at home: Dad with Evangelia, Dad with Rhodou, Dad with Eugenia. He didn't mind. In fact, he loved it, and carried out these duties wearing the beaming smile we all remember him by.

After the church and the photos, everyone would arrive at the reception, but instead of us sitting at a table as a family, Dad would go to the kitchen to help dish out. Buffets didn't seem to have been invented back then, so each guest's plate was prepared by the men in the kitchen and placed in front of them by another team of men. On every table would be bottles of Johnnie Walker, Commandaria, Cypriot brandy and beer.

Musicians played in the background, and once everyone was fed and suitably watered it was time to get up and dance. It is customary at weddings to have Cypriot musicians who play traditional music. In the old days they used to perform throughout the evening, but as the Cypriots became more westernised they introduced "European" music to the celebrations: a guitarist, a drummer and sometimes an accordionist. They usually played some tango tunes, cha-cha, rumba and even rock and roll. Their renditions made us kids cringe: hearing them singing English with heavy Cypriot accents was hilarious. Edmundo Ros's *Wedding Samba* was considered very daring, but it got the crowds up on their feet. Girls danced with girls, as dancing with boys was generally frowned upon by our strict parents.

The festivities would continue into the night, with everyone getting progressively merrier. Sometimes the high spirits degenerated into drunken brawls. Back in the days of weddings at the Glory, Jo and I often saw grown men throwing punches at each other while stumbling around on the pavement blind drunk. I would be terrified of Dad getting involved, but I needn't have worried. The most he would do was try to placate them, but of course all he got was a stream of verbal abuse.

The highlight of the wedding celebrations is undoubtedly the traditional dance. This is when guests pin money on the bride and groom. It's a tradition that began back in the remote villages of Cyprus, where there were no shops to buy a proper present and it was easier just to give cash. Musicians strike up the tune of *Ayia Stolliste Tin Kala* (Dress Up the Bride Well) and the dancing couple are descended upon by the hordes. Tradition has it that the parents pin first, then the siblings, then grandparents and so on.

Back in the day, the usual amount was a £1 note on both the bride and the groom. Now it's a real show of wealth. Parents spend hours before the big day pinning notes together into a kind of concertina. They approach the couple with their huge stack, pin the top note on a shoulder and let the rest cascade like a waterfall to reveal tens of £50 notes. Once that's done, friends and family get up and continue the pinning. Couples can reap thousands of pounds in this way. I once turned up at a relative's house in Cyprus three days after their wedding; they emerged bleary-eyed having just finished counting £60,000!

But there's a growing trend among third and fourth generation Cypriot kids, who are becoming ever more anglicised, for these old traditions to be discarded. These days the violinist is lucky to get a walk-on part, hovering backstage like a forgotten stand-up act. The bride and groom preferring wedding lists to the money dance and music played by hip DJ's while professional lighting and cameramen record the happy event.

When did weddings become so glitzy, so lavish and so professionally put together? I remember my parents telling me that in London in 1938, when they got married, one of their presents was a bottle of olive oil (probably a naughty joke) but that's how poor people were back then.

'Ο Κος ΤΑΚΗΣ ΚΥΡΙΑΚΟΥ

'Εκ Κώμης Κεπὴρ

ΚΑΙ

ἡ Δνὶς ΔΕΣΠΩ ΧΡΥΣΟΣΤΟΜΟΥ ΚΩΣΤΗ

'Εκ Κάμπου

θὰ εὐχαριστηθοῦν πολὺ ἐὰν παρευρεθῆτε μετὰ τῆς ἀξιοτίμου οἰκογενείας σας εἰς τοὺς γάμους των, τελεσθησομένους τὴν Κυριακήν, 21ην Μαρτίου, 1965, καὶ ὥραν 4.30 μ.μ. εἰς τὴν 'Ορθόδοξον 'Ελληνικὴν 'Εκκλησίαν 'Αγίων Πάντων, PRATT STREET, CAMDEN TOWN, N.W.1.

Μετὰ τὴν τέλεσιν τοῦ μυστηρίου οἱ προσκεκλημένοι θὰ μεταφερθοῦν μὲ λεωφορεῖα στὴν δεξίωσιν FRIARS HALL 236, Blackfriars Road S.E.1.

Mr TAKIS KYRIACOU

AND

Miss DESPO CHRISOSTOMOU COSTI

request the pleasure of your company at their wedding on Sunday 21st March, 1965, at 1.30 p.m., in the Greek Orthodox Church All Saints, Pratt Street, Camden Town, N.W.1.

After the ceremony, coaches will take the guests to the Wedding reception, at FRIARS HALL 236, Blackfriars Road S.E.1.

Wedding invitation, 1965

Kyriacos and Georgoulla's wedding, All Saint, Camden 1951

Cousin Evangelia with Dad, who walked her down the aisle at All Saints church in Pratt Street Camden,1955

Mihalis and Nina Engomitis, with me and Helen as bridesmaids. According to Mum, "Edaizes ena gharon" (You could feed a whole donkey on the bouquets back then)

Dad before walking cousin Eugenia down the aisle, with Koulla as bridesmaid. St Mary's church, Wood Green, 1982

Dessi Skoutari on her wedding day, London, 1959

Cousin Stavroulla and husband Varvarakis with a lot of money on their wedding day in Cyprus

PRATT STREET

The first place babies were taken to after being brought home from the maternity ward was the Greek Orthodox Church, where they were blessed at 40 days old. I don't know if Orthodox babies today are not given an airing before 40 days, but back then it was the norm. The tradition is known as posarantosis: a blessing is bestowed upon the newborn, together with its mother, that emulates the Virgin Mary taking Jesus into the Temple 40 days after his birth. Prayers and thanks are said for the safe arrival of the infant, who is formally presented to the Church.

I was taken to All Saints in Pratt Street, Camden. Pratt Street, as we referred to the church, played a large part in my life, but not always for reasons of devotion. As a small child I went there most Sundays, usually with Dad as Mum had to stay behind to cook the obligatory Sunday roast. Of course, I couldn't understand much of what was going on, but I was fascinated by the theatricality and the heady smell of incense – at that age, it was a bit like being taken to Oxford Street to see the Christmas lights. The other kids and I would end up playing in the pews. Greeks seem to view church as a bit of a social meeting place and there's always chatter and noise, while the priest carries on as if he can't see or hear his unruly congregation. I was always amused by the worshippers who loudly greeted each other during the service, and went on to discuss their health, wealth and business ventures.

Weddings, christenings, funerals and memorials: there have been thousands at Pratt Street. We would take the bus from Howland Street or Tottenham Court Road, up along Hampstead Road and past the art deco Craven A cigarette factory with its statuesque black cats – always a source of childhood fascination. Invariably we would bump into other friends and family at the bus stop, and a row would break out about who would pay the fares: "No, it's my turn!" "No, it's *my* turn, you paid the last time. I'm not going to talk to you any more." I felt sorry for the bus conductor. He would have to wait patiently until somebody won the argument and paid the round of fares. Things were momentarily peaceful, but soon the churchgoers would find something amusing and the bus was once again filled with shrieks and laughter.

After the church service was over, we would file outside and be greeted by more friends and family. This would take forever: cheeks were kissed, extended family were asked after. How was the business going? Was there any news from Cyprus? When was young Maria getting married? Minutes would then be spent negotiating the invitations to lunch. Before finally heading off, people would queue to buy the Greek savouries on sale at various stalls in the church grounds. It was more like a bazaar than a church; any feelings of divine spirituality were quickly replaced by gluttony.

We didn't like those food stalls too much, but Dad often

stopped at the one that sold seafood. He would buy a pint of winkles and bring them home, where we would pick them out of their tiny shells with a needle. I really liked eating them, but only until my sister remarked that they looked like snot. The thought of eating snot put me off forever and I haven't touched a winkle since. Poor Dad would always come in for a hard time from Mum, when she saw the candle wax he had carelessly allowed to drip on his hat and coat while in deep spiritual reverie. He would sit there taking the lecture, wearing a cheesy grin, until she cleaned his clothes and normality returned. Until the following week, when we would go through the same thing all over again.

One of the most memorable church incidents happened one Easter, after the Resurrection service on the Saturday night, the most important date in the Orthodox calendar. This always starts at 10pm and the Resurrection is an hour later. It's a very colourful service and not to be missed – these days it's usually the only one I go to all year. It contains some utterly spine-tingling moments, and even if you think the whole thing is a nonsense you can't help but be moved.

Jo and I had gone along with Mum while Dad was working, and the church was teeming. Towards the end of the service the lights were switched off, as tradition dictates, and a feeling of anticipation spread among the flock. In the darkened church, the sound of the liturgy was heard from behind the iconostasis (a partition where icons are displayed). A few minutes passed and then the priests, shimmering in their gold embroidered vestments, came forth bearing aloft five candles each, two in one hand, three in the other. The candles were lit with what, we were told, was a flame brought all the way from Christ's tomb at the Church of the Holy Sepulchre in Jerusalem. The chanting reached its climax when the words "Christos Anesti" (Christ has Risen) were uttered, and with that the flame from the priests' candles was passed around the entire congregation, until each of us held our own candle lit from Jerusalem, the holiest of places.

So, Christ had risen and it was time to catch the bus home. My mother and a few other brave souls had no intention of blowing their candles out – they would be taking them home to light the pilot on the stove, thereby ensuring the house was lit with the flame from Christ's tomb all year round. But they hadn't reckoned on the no-nonsense conductor on the no. 253 bus. This was back in the late 60s and he must have been the first to practise health and safety. "You're not bringing that candle on to my bus," he said. "Iss my relligio," Mum protested. "I don't care what it is," he fired back. After a five-minute standoff, the other passengers had stopped thinking it was funny and started to shift in their seats. The conductor, by now really pissed off, jumped off the bus and went to speak to the driver, who switched the engine off and just sat there. We all did, for ages. Who was going to give in first? Of course, it was us. Dejected but defiant, we clambered off the bus with our candles still alight and waited until a friendly taxi driver picked us up. He didn't care about having a naked flame in the back of his cab. And so we arrived home, the pilot was relit and we had holy light for another year. All was well with the world.

One thing that has stayed true in all these years is the tradition of the Orthodox liturgy. It is considered the world's oldest Christian service and what is so great, in my opinion, is that nothing has changed over the years. The service is the same today as it was back in the fourth century, at the time of St John Chrysostomou. It is also interesting that no musical instruments are used, only the human voice, which is considered the perfect vehicle.

My first photo! With Mum at Regent's Park after my 40-day ceremony at All Saints church, Camden

With my Godfather Tata Takis at my christening

My family outside All Saints church, Camden

Outside All Saints: after cousin Stavros's christening. Mum is Godmother

THE BEAUTIFUL GAME

We weren't fanatical, but my family did like to watch a game of football. We had a little black and white TV in the kitchen that my parents bought when I was 16 – it would flicker and jump and the picture was grainy, but we thought it was the bee's knees. After our roast lunch on Sundays, our afternoon ritual was that I would make Greek coffees and we'd settle in for the match. It was one of the few chances Mum had to put her feet up: she would make herself comfortable in one of the wooden chairs, but after about 10 minutes she would nod off. My parents, for completely emotional reasons, supported Manchester United. They felt huge sympathy for them after the 1958 plane crash in Munich, in which eight players and three staffers lost their lives. For Mum and Dad, it was good enough reason to cheer the team on.

London Cypriots are mainly divided into two camps: Arsenal fans and Spurs fans. Many moved to North London when they made a bit of money and bought their first homes, and those were the North London teams of choice. But my preference was shaped by my cousin Simos, Sooty's dad. As a carpenter, Simos worked mostly in Fulham for big companies like Taylor Woodrow and McAlpine, and he had two obvious teams to choose from: Fulham or Chelsea. Simos chose Chelsea and so did I. He became a True Blue, supporting them until his dying day, and his relatives even placed the Chelsea flag over his grave in Cyprus. Before he died in 1998, Simos had made his family promise that should his team win anything significant in the years to come, they would not forget him. His wish was fulfilled in 2005. Chelsea won the Premiership under the management of José Mourinho, and the Champions flag was brought to Cyprus and draped over his final resting place.

Simos had enjoyed many Saturdays at the Shed End, in the days when the working man could afford the price of a ticket and the players were paid not much more than office workers. He would take Sooty along with him, and where Sooty went, I usually went too. My recollections of Stamford Bridge back then are not so much of the games but of the backs of men's legs. Everyone in those days stood to watch the match, and Sooty and I, aged five and seven, were still quite small. And then there was the swaying. Whole sections of supporters would sway, depending on where the ball was going, just to get a better look. I still can't believe more injuries weren't sustained on those Saturday afternoons.

The worst thing to happen to us at the Bridge was when Sooty's mum threw up on the back of an unsuspecting man's legs – and then wiped him down. I don't think he even noticed and, in disbelief, we carried on watching the game as though nothing had happened. Getting to the Bridge was a bit of a pain, even from central London, so the introduction of the TV to our lives was a blessing. Who would want to tube it over to Fulham when you could watch from home? Plenty do, but not me.

Of course, the TV came into its own for the World Cup final at Wembley in 1966. What a game that was! The excitement in our house was tangible and we all sat on the edges of our seats until that final, beautiful whistle. England winning the World Cup was amazing and unbelievable. I ran out on to the street and jumped up and down with joy; the neighbours came out to join me, laughing and shouting. Upstairs, Panagis could be heard whooping his crazy head off.

Then, in 1973, football royalty walked into our house in the delightful form of Shirley Wale, the fiancée of my Godbrother Douglas. Shirley's dad was Sidney Wale, the chairman of Spurs, who was a true gent, very much like Douglas's dad, Uncle Avgousti. The Wale connection with the club started with Shirley's grandfather Fred, a local businessman who joined the board in 1942. Douglas himself joined the board of directors in June 1980 and was chairman from 1982–84, during which time Spurs won the 1984 UEFA Cup against Anderlecht, as well as various FA Cups. Douglas recalls drinking champagne from the FA Cup after one of their wins and spilling it on his Spurs scarf, after which he didn't ever want to wash it. More recently, Spurs played against the Cypriot side APOEL in a Champions League game at Wembley, beating them 3–0, which must have toyed with Douglas's loyalties.

I still enjoy watching the game, although I haven't been to a live match for years. My husband is a huge West Ham fan so I now live in a divided household. I confess I've got a bit of a soft spot for the Hammers, although I do get a bit tired of being told they won the World Cup for us. I know three of their players were in the victorious England side, including the captain, Bobby Moore, but even so…

Over the years a few Chelsea matches have stood out for me, including the second leg of the Champion's League match against Barcelona in 2005, when we won 4-2, 5-4 on aggregate. That must rate as the most exciting game I've ever seen. I actually couldn't bring myself to watch the last crucial moments: my dear friend George Petri and I stood with our backs to the stadium, our hearts in our mouths, waiting for the telltale roar, which happily came loud and strong towards the end. The coldest I've ever been was at a Chelsea game against Leeds one freezing winter's day in the 90s. I wondered why I ever chose to spend my Saturday afternoons chilled to the core watching 22 grown men kicking a silly ball around. But there you go, that's football.

Douglas, then a Spurs director, holding the FA Cup after the team won the trophy in 1981

Douglas, then Chairman of Spurs, holding the UEFA Cup after the team's victory on 23 May 1984 (the eve of his birthday!)

Luke with his parents Sooty and George, outside the Matthew Harding stand at Stamford Bridge after Chelsea won the Premiership in 2005

Simos's grave in Cyprus covered with Chelsea Champions flag, 2005

POCKET MONEY

When I was at primary school, I used to get threepence a week in pocket money. Amazingly, that threepence bought a healthy (or not) supply of sweets and comics: Black Jacks and Fruit Salad chews were four a penny, Mr Marks's oily, broken crisps on Foley Street were a farthing, and comics were fourpence. My favourites were *Bunty* and *Judy*, and I'd read them cover to cover in one sitting.

On one occasion when I was about eight, the newsagent had sold out of *Bunty*. This was a disaster. I hatched a plan that involved my going over to Sooty's to see if she had a copy – she had, but she hadn't read it yet, so I sat in her house for an hour until she finished it. This was in the days before we had a telephone, so Mum was left to imagine the worst. When I arrived home, clutching Sooty's *Bunty*, Mum hit the proverbial roof. She'd been worried sick and I got the telling-off of my life, which I was half expecting but couldn't really understand. I knew I was OK, so why was she so worried? It didn't make sense. Besides, why didn't my parents have a phone like everyone else?

We were always given something for Christmas and

birthdays. My favourite of all was a large and rather gaudy-looking doll that we christened Jeanne-Pierette. Or rather, my sister did, being in the middle of her "French period", as we called it. I would have preferred Jane or Linda, but no, the doll had to be Jeanne-Pierette. JP had platinum plaits, red lipstick and wore a blue dress, and if you turned her on to her belly she cried "Mama" which, come to think of it, did sound rather French. I also had a much-loved doll called Charlie, named after Prince Charles. To me, he was sweetness personified; he was dressed in a shiny yellow romper suit and looked like a real baby.

Most of my toys and games were bought for me by my parents or relatives. We were never spoiled. If Mum, who we went shopping with, decided we couldn't afford something, it was a firm "no" and no amount of arguing would change her mind. We had some colossal fights. There was a huge row when I had outgrown a coat and hated its style as well – I wanted a new one but she refused point blank, saying there was nothing wrong with the one I had. Well, I wouldn't hear of it and went into a hormonal rage, refusing to wear the coat, refusing to go to a family wedding, refusing to leave the house and tearing at my stockings like some mad banshee. In the end I was completely spent. I've no idea how Mum felt but she didn't give in – she was as obstinate as a Cypriot donkey.

Maddeningly for me, I was always the one who had to say sorry first. Mum was better than me at giving the cold shoulder and could carry on for days as though I wasn't there. My plate of food would appear on the table, but otherwise I was invisible. She was the boss, but I could push her to her limits and often did.

THE DOCTOR AND THE DENTIST

There was only one doctor for us and that was Dr Panizzi – or Banezi, as my parents called him. There was a GP around the corner from us in Candover Street, but for some reason my parents didn't like Dr Berman and so they chose Dr Panizzi – probably because he was Italian, the nearest thing to being Greek, in their eyes. His practice was in Devonshire Place, off Harley Street near Regent's Park, which was quite a trek for me as a child. As a teenager I was quite happy to walk the 15 minutes, because I could detour past 57 Wimpole Street in the hope of seeing my favourite Beatle, Paul McCartney. He lived there with his then girlfriend, Jane Asher, and her family. I never did see him, though I always thought I could feel the vibes and hear the song *Yesterday*, which was apparently composed in that house. It made my visits to the doctor that much more bearable.

The closest I got to Paul was seeing Gordon Waller outside the Ashers' home when I was 15. He was part of the singing duo Peter and Gordon, and Peter was the brother of Jane Asher, so that made it a couple of degrees of separation better in my eyes. Gordon was sitting in his red Mini outside the house and I spotted him as I made my way to the doctor's surgery, but I had a terrible pain and didn't want to stop. We had one of those smiley, wavey exchanges and I thought he was very good-looking – but still, he wasn't Paul.

Onwards to the surgery. Dr Panizzi had a couple of dark, dusty rooms that were so gloomy I swear they made you feel worse than any medical condition. Despite this, my parents thought he was God. Most of his patients were migrants and most of them thought the same. Italian by birth, Dr Panizzi was a miracle worker and something of a maverick. Gruff by nature, waxy of skin and always with a fag in his hand, he looked like he could do with seeing a doctor himself, yet he treated us with a lot of success and without too much fuss or discussion. What always surprised me was that my parents tipped him at the end of their visits. I can't remember exactly how much it was, but he accepted it without hesitation, putting it straight into his trouser pocket. Surely you can't do this if you're an NHS doctor? Then again, he was a maverick and no one got hurt.

In those days we had home visits, and Dr Panizzi would come and see us if we were too ill to get out of our sick beds. This was often the case with childhood illnesses like chicken pox and measles. My parents, having to go out to work, would be forced to leave me alone in the flat, hoping I would manage to sleep through any temperature and trusting I wouldn't spend too much time scratching those itchy spots. It wasn't a decision they took lightly, and I know Mum really worried about leaving me alone, but they didn't have much choice. Sooty's mum would occasionally look in, but she too had her work and I suspect she didn't want to pick up anything contagious to take home to Sooty. I don't recall illnesses being too much of a hardship, just very uncomfortable. What I remember most are the injections and the trauma afterwards. The needles seemed to be a foot long and the pain would last forever.

Years later, my first husband, Edward, developed quite a large lump on the back of his right hand. Despite several visits to doctors, no medicine or cream would get rid of it, and he was pretty desperate when my parents suggested he visit Dr Panizzi. I went with him. We sat down opposite the good doctor, who examined Edward's hand and then went across to his library of books. He came back with what must have been the biggest and heaviest of his medical tomes and asked Edward to put his hand out on the desk. Dr Panizzi then brought the weighty volume down hard on Edward's hand and to our surprise the lump disappeared, just like that. We couldn't believe it. Dr Panizzi laughed and shrugged his shoulders – and then we too gave him a tip, which he happily pocketed. Despite the curious tipping, he was much loved.

Not so the dentist – I don't think there was anyone who liked him. Mine were very good teeth, but I did need a filling, so I was lined up to see the school dentist. I sat in the chair, which was positioned facing a window looking out over the street, and a purple contraption was placed over my nose. I was then told to breathe in. I remember the gas and the smell, and the excruciating pain and hot tears that followed. I felt the overwhelming desire to be anywhere else in the world, to be any one of those people walking along Foley Street, who I could see as I sat there in the torture chamber. This left me with a fear of dentists and I didn't seek another one out for the next 20 years. During that time, one of my wisdom teeth fell to pieces and my bottom teeth became crooked and snagged. I blame that shyster dentist.

LANGUAGE AND LEARNING

My sister and I always spoke Greek at home with our parents, and with the endless stream of aunts, uncles and neighbours who visited us. It was my mother tongue and thank goodness it was, because trying to learn it years later would have been a challenge, to say the least.

Our parents' grasp of English was average, but better than a lot of their contemporaries. They taught themselves to read and they could also write, although that was fairly limited. Both had been taken out of school at an early age, Mum at nine and Dad at 11. He was distraught when this happened – he was very good at school and loved learning, but he was an only son and Grandpa needed him to work the fields.

Their spoken English wasn't bad, but their pronunciation was sometimes so skewed it was almost a new language in itself. Oxford Street became Ofxo Stri, Great Titchfield Street was Gray Chiffi Stri, Goodge Street, Goosh Stri, Tottenham Court Road, Totteha Koh Roh, Finsbury Park, Fishbury Paak, Regent's Park was Rigess Paak and Trafalgar Square became the tongue-twisting Trafasga Skuea. Weirdest of all, the pub, or public house, became the "bobligao". Jo and I would try to correct them but they just couldn't get it.

Despite being born in London, I didn't learn to speak English until about the age of four. But from primary school onwards, English became my language of choice. I would speak it to my sister and to friends but, interestingly, never to my parents – I would naturally switch to Greek and that continued until they died. Jo and I would also flip to Greek to say something we didn't want our English friends to understand.

The next step for me was to learn to read English – and then, of course, to read Greek. My sister took over the job of teaching me. I don't remember reading being a hard thing to do: kids can absorb most of what is thrown at them and learning to read in my second language, English, which actually became my first, felt easy and natural. As was learning to read in Greek, even though it is complex and the alphabet is made up of weird-looking symbols.

Later, when she was 17, my sister won a scholarship to study languages at the French Lycée in South Kensington and from then on our house became truly tricolore. We listened to the pop music show *Salut les Copains* on the radio and read French magazines, *Paris Match* being the weekly favourite (in the West End every newsagent stocked non-English newspapers and magazines, so they were never a problem to buy). Thanks to Jo, I grew up listening to Johnny Hallyday, Sylvie Vartan, Enrico Macias, Adamo and my favourite singer of all, Françoise Hardy. She was my style icon – I grew my hair long and cut a fringe so I could look like her. I sang just as well in French as I did in Greek and English, and Jo and I felt a little superior to everyone else as we considered ourselves truly Continental!

Jo's enthusiasm and her teaching instinct helped me with my studies. When I was still at primary school she made a little book of elementary French vocabulary for me. She sewed the spine with blue cotton to make sure the pages didn't fall out and divided each page into four sections, with each containing a picture and a description in French: underneath a drawing of a cat she wrote "le chat", for example, while a car was "la voiture". This gave me a head start in the language and I should have excelled, but I was a lazy pupil who daydreamed of boys and the Beatles.

We were very lucky to have a good library nearby in Little Titchfield Street. I would spend hours going through all the books and deciding which ones to take home. My favourites were the usual children's classics but with a preference for adventure: The Famous Five, The Secret Seven, Jennings and Derbyshire, Biggles. One book that I read when I was about seven affected me quite badly. I've forgotten the title, but it told the tale of a little pet dog that was run over and killed. I cried so much over that dog that I think Mum grew worried about my state of mind; I remember her trying to reason with me, telling me not to be silly and it was only a book, but it made no difference. The grief in my seven-year-old heart for that little dog was enormous and real.

Much of my reading was done sitting at the kitchen table. In later years I did my revision in the same spot, though I don't know how I managed to retain any information among all the clatter and chatter. In 1962, when I was revising for my exams, the house was full of people who had come to see Dad before he sailed to Cyprus on holiday with my sister. Back then it was usual for friends and relatives, and even strangers, to turn up before someone was travelling and give them money to take to family back home. On this occasion, Dad ended up with hundreds of pounds in envelopes marked with different names. Not only was this probably illegal, but it also meant he had to spend half his holiday traipsing around trying to find these people.

But that wasn't my problem. Mine was where I was going to revise. The kitchen was crammed full of people for days on end, and so was the upstairs sitting room. There were people sitting all over my bed, so I couldn't even use my bedroom. In desperation and ignored by the masses, who were all having a great time laughing and drinking tea, I took my books and sat on the stairs on the second floor. I felt miserable and frustrated, and I used that as an excuse when I passed only four subjects out of 10 that year.

HIGH SCHOOL

My sister was academically bright and, if I'm honest, I probably got into grammar school because of her. She was a natural swot and they must have thought I was one, too. I managed to pass my 11-plus, though I hadn't a clue what I was doing or how life-changing this test would be. I went into it completely unprepared, having revised nothing – in fact, I didn't even know what the word revision meant. My parents were in no position to guide me and on this occasion even my "teacher" sister failed to convey the importance of the educational crossroads ahead of me.

But pass I did, so the obvious choice was to try to get into Jo's grammar, Paddington and Maida Vale High School for Girls. Miraculously, I did get in and there was much celebration in our house. The school's motto was "praevalebit veritas", meaning "truth shall prevail", though in truth, I don't know how I got there.

I was born in August, so I was a very young 11-year old in September 1960 when I embarked on the next phase of my life. Friends from All Souls came with me on that journey – and in the literal sense. Sandra Dashwood lived around the corner in Nassau Street and each morning we made our way to school together. Over the next couple of years our twosome became a foursome. We were joined by Sooty and by Helen, another childhood friend who had passed her 11-plus.

Sooty was the first of our pack to set off in the mornings. She lived in Great Titchfield Street and picked me up from Riding House Street. Next we went to Sandra's in Nassau Street and finally to Helen's in Wells Street. We would then walk at a snail's pace to Oxford Circus and wait for the no. 6 bus, which took us to Maida Vale; we disembarked at the Shirland Road stop and walked the short distance to school on Elgin Avenue. Our aim was to catch the 8.10am bus to get us to school for 8.45am, in time for assembly at 9am. Somehow, we always made it.

One day we were halfway to picking up Helen when one of my hold-up stockings fell down. Hold-ups were the new "in" thing, but back then they were crap at staying up. I was hugely embarrassed and my predicament triggered shrieks of laughter from my friends. It was a winter's day and I couldn't go to school bare-legged, so I returned home and changed into tights. I used this lame excuse when I arrived at school half an hour late and was given lines and detention for my trouble.

We were forever larking around on the journey, and if we weren't falling about laughing we were eyeing up the boys. I also had a passion for the newly released Jaguar E-type and would stand ogling if one were to drive by. In the West End there were a fair number of Jags and I would count how many I saw.

Our journey home was often even more insane. We acted

like inmates who had just been released from prison. Looking back, I feel sorry for the passersby and bus passengers we terrorised – not intentionally, of course, but even so, I cringe when I think of how loud we were and how stupidly we behaved. Never more so than the time we were flashed on the top deck of the bus. The four of us were getting ready to get off at Oxford Circus when there, at the top of the stairs, appeared a vile little man waving his willy at us. He looked manic and ridiculous. He was wearing a grey mac, a hat and thick round spectacles, like a relic from the 50s. We screamed, laughed and chased him down the stairs shouting "Catch that man!" to all and sundry. Unfortunately, no one took any notice and he disappeared into the crowd never to be seen again, at least by us.

Our spirits were usually high and nothing deterred us from messing around. There was a trick we often played that we thought was hilarious. We would go into a public telephone box, dial the operator and as soon as she answered we'd say, "Get off the line, there's a train coming!" How silly was that? We fell about laughing every time.

The six years I spent at high school were generally very happy. The curriculum was quite tough and I did OK, though I could have done better, as my school reports always seemed to suggest. As well as being a bit of a dreamer, I made friends with girls who weren't overly studious and so I ended up in class X as opposed to class A. There were three streams in each year, A, X and Y, and A was for the brightest girls. They took Latin and usually went on to university. Girls in my class got pregnant at 11 and took purple hearts, the drug of choice back in the 60s.

I was fast becoming a mod. First my hair was very short, then long and dark with a heavy fringe, just like my hero, Cathy McGowan on the TV music show *Ready Steady Go*. Music was taking over our lives and we had little time for schoolwork. Small shops called "boutiques" were opening up all over the West End, while Carnaby Street in Soho was becoming the place to shop and be seen. How I managed to steer my way through school and pass any exam is a mystery. I ended up cramming, like most of my friends, spending hours and hours revising each night and realising, far too late, that my future was about to be determined.

Barbara Edwards, Anne de Rago and me outside our house, 57 Riding House Street

Paddington & Maida Vale High School photo, 1961: I'm in the front row, second from left

High school chums larking around. Me with Valerie Davies, far right, 1964

With high school chums, me far right with ice lolly, 1965

RAG TRADE FRIENDS

The area around where we lived was known as the rag trade. Every other shop and factory seemed to have something to do with dressmaking, or "schmutter". That's also true today, though to a lesser degree. Of course, to a fashion-mad teenager such as me it was like living in heaven. My school friend Helen would call round and together we would drop into the nearby clothing workshops, shamelessly asking what they had at discount prices. No one seemed to mind and we spent hours going through the stock choosing our next dress. We usually paid something like a fiver. Later, we would see the same dress being sold at Wallis on Oxford Street for £20 and feel really pleased with ourselves.

Helen and I spent a lot of time together. I went to her place every Monday after doing my homework and she came over to me on Tuesdays. It's a mystery why we didn't space out our visits. But we always had plenty to talk about and even more to laugh about, and it's still the same today – we usually collapse into a heap within five minutes of meeting up.

I liked going over to Helen's. Her family's flat was better designed than ours and about 100 years newer. They had their own toilet, which they kept locked and was off the communal hallway, not out in the backyard like ours. They also had a proper bath, which was in the kitchen and covered with a lid, so you never knew it was there. Their living room and two bedrooms were rather small, much smaller than ours, so at least we were ahead on that score.

Helen's flat was also the closest to Oxford Street, by about two minutes, so that induced more envy. She and her sister Lulla, who was roughly the same age as Jo, would arrive home and dump their shopping bags, while we had another couple of blocks to schlep before we could offload ours. They were also closest to Bourne & Hollingsworth, our favourite shop. B&H was one of the first department stores to open on Oxford Street, way back in 1902. Once, when one of their windows had a display of vacuum cleaners, Helen's little nephew Kyriacos developed an obsession with them and would cry until someone took him to look at them. He would stand there for ages, repeating the word "Hoover" over and over until patience wore thin and he was dragged back home again. No prizes for guessing his nickname.

FAMILY HOLIDAYS

Although my parents were working class and didn't have much money, they understood the need for holidays. Dad worked under intense pressure as a chef, six days a week, 51 weeks a year. Anyone who has watched *MasterChef* will know how insane the pace is in restaurant kitchens. Mum worked just as hard in the rag trade, tailoring suits for wealthy women. She also did all the cooking, cleaning and raised us virtually single-handed. To say they must have been knackered is an understatement. As well as a rest, they also needed to get out of the West End, to breathe in some fresh air and look at the sky.

Our early holidays were to seaside resorts such as Brighton and Bognor Regis. In those days we had no phone and no way of booking rooms at a bed and breakfast, so Dad would head off the previous Sunday to whichever resort we'd decided on, and go from house to house until he found something suitable. After securing the booking, he would catch the train home again and give us the good news.

On the first morning of the holiday, always a Saturday, Mum would get up at the crack of dawn and prepare sandwiches for the journey. She would pack our bags, including the blow-up beach ball, the bucket and spade, and Dad's khaki trousers and sandals (so he could imagine he was in Cyprus). The last job was to turf out the cat. I can't imagine this happening today. Poor Kitty, or Ginger, or whoever the cat of the moment was would be put out on the street, with a promise from a neighbour that they would feed it. Who knows whether they did or not, but our cats usually turned up to greet us when we returned.

Of course, with no phone, it was Dad's job to find a taxi to take us to the station. He usually got lucky on Mortimer Street, jumping in and swinging by the house to pick us up before heading off to Victoria. The train journey was very exciting and part of the magic of going on holiday. It was the golden age of travel: steam trains would transport hardworking Londoners and their families away from the grime and filth to the fun of the seaside. I can still smell the trains, and hear them; there was such romance about those big, beautiful beasts. Their carriages were usually divided into compartments that seated six to eight people, with a narrow corridor that allowed passengers to walk the length of the train. We would find an empty compartment, pile in and make ourselves comfortable. Dad was in charge of the baggage: he would heave it on to the luggage racks overhead and then settle down for a well-deserved puff on his pipe.

Then we were off, snaking our way past inner-city houses covered in black soot and towards the green fields of our dreams. We were full of anticipation and so was Dad. He would always point out the obvious along the way: "Look, sheep!" or "Did you see those cows?" Yes, Dad.

Brighton was our family's favourite destination, and we even went there for the occasional day out. The view of the sea from Brighton station was one of the most exciting things I had witnessed as a child. It still gives me a tingle, the way the horizon is set quite high up, with the road from the station dipping down towards it.

We would search for our B&B, hoping that Dad could remember where it was. There were a few close calls, but most of the time we managed to find the guest house and check in. They always smelled and it was not a very nice smell either: a mixture of dog, boiled food and stuffy air. Almost immediately we would grab our things and head off to the sea. What a glorious feeling. Jo and I would spend all day swimming and building sandcastles, while our parents hired deck chairs and snoozed. Dad, who was quite fair, got serious sunstroke one year after falling asleep and was off work for days. We would also forage for wild food and eat seafood plucked fresh from the sea. Dad's favourites were the limpets that he prised off the rocks and ate while they were still alive, which to us girls was horrid.

In those days, Brighton had a wonderful paddling pool for kids. I would splash about in it and turn a very dark brown. Mum used to look at me and say, "Ra Hele, ise o Gandis", likening me to Mahatma Gandhi because I was so thin and brown. Despite her lack of schooling, she was no slouch when it came to naming world leaders.

The only blot on my landscape was eating in public. It was charming, really, but Dad used to get into a pickle when dining in restaurants. He was naturally very clumsy and always dropped his peas – they would fall off his fork and roll on to the table and the floor. My sister would get embarrassed and have a go at him, which made things even worse. It was the same at breakfast: Dad's sausage fingers were more used to picking food out of frying pans than handling utensils in public.

There came a time when the seaside guest house was replaced by the caravan. It was our neighbours on the ground floor, Annie and Kounti, who first enlightened us. Annie, who was Welsh, would talk enthusiastically about holidaying in Snowdonia and how marvellous it was to be in a self-contained mobile home away from strict landladies. My parents were sold. The attractions of fresh mountain air far outweighed the downsides of do-it-yourself holidays where you had to cook, wash and do all the cleaning. That was Mum's job: it wasn't enough that she cleaned Riding House Street all year round, but she also had to scrub her temporary home. She didn't seem to mind. One caravan owner even wrote and thanked her for leaving the blasted thing so spotlessly clean.

Those holidays were really very special. I could actually see my parents unwinding as they sat and looked at the breathtaking Welsh scenery. They would always say that the crystal clear waterfalls, wide open spaces and simple way of life reminded them of their village back in Cyprus. Food tasted a hundred times better in Wales, too. We would pick up produce from farms and make salads in the evenings that were so fresh and flavoursome they put the goods from Berwick Street market to shame. Sadly, these country sojourns brought home to us that for most of the time, our life in the Big Smoke meant we were just making do.

In July 1963, when I was almost 14 and we were holidaying

in North Wales, I spotted a poster: "The Beatles in concert, Ritz Ballroom, Rhyl." I couldn't sleep that night. I was a huge Beatles fan and I just *had* to see them. Well, we managed to get tickets and I went with my sister to my very first Beatles concert. How can I even begin to describe it? The place was electric. Of course, you couldn't hear a thing over the screaming: the fans yelled, cried, tore at their hair, while I sat dumbfounded, in shock at being in the same room as my heroes. Wales may be a lot of things to a lot of people, but to me it's where I first saw the Beatles.

Cornwall became another family favourite and we would travel down to Fowey and Mevagissey in search of wild food and sun. There were plenty of both, but there was also a fair amount of rain. Undeterred, my father would wait for the storms to blow over and head off with a bucket to forage for supper. Snails were everywhere: under rocks, on top of rocks and crawling through the grass. Dad would come back with a bucketful, alive and kicking with their antennae waving about. But not for long, because the kettle would be boiled and the poor snails would be scalded alive. Jo and I would rather have starved than eat a snail, but our parents scoffed them straight from the shells with a little salt and pepper. None of this poncey garlic butter for them.

One caravan holiday was so traumatic that it lingers like a wound in my family's collective memory. We had decided to go to the south coast, to Selsey, with Sooty and her parents. Sooty and I had grown into stroppy adolescents by then, me more than her. We had also become embarrassed to be on holiday with our parents and this added to the toxic mix. The two of us came to blows virtually every day: we would scream and yell and pull at each other's hair, as our parents looked on in horror. In my head, Sooty was to blame for all my teenage angst, and so I let her have it. While we screamed at each other, our respective mothers screamed at us. It reached a point where I thought our parents would fall out; we had turned their so-called holiday into two weeks of hell. Thankfully, their friendship and close family ties won out over a couple of neurotic schoolgirls who took their frustrations out on each other. Ten out of 10 for being such wise old Greeks, and 10 out of 10 to Sooty and me for still being good friends today.

A couple of years after the Selsey debacle, Jo and I went to Spain – our first overseas destination that wasn't Cyprus – with Sooty, her parents and our friend Thalia. Mum and Dad stayed at home in London, so Sooty's parents were in charge of three teenagers and my older sister. For us, Spain promised sun, sea, boys and, most of all, freedom. We wanted to have fun, though Sooty, two years younger than me, was still tethered to her mum and dad and couldn't join in with us older ones. The trip must have been a nightmare for Sooty's parents. They still held the Cypriot belief that young girls shouldn't be let out of sight, whereas all we wanted to do was disappear. But it was their holiday as well and we must have been a real pain for them, while poor Sooty was torn between obeying her parents and hanging out with the "rebels".

There were days when we would all go to the beach and even eat together, but most of the time us girls would find an excuse to go off on our own. Sooty's parents wouldn't have wanted to criticise us too much, out of respect for my parents, but I'm sure they thought we were devils incarnate. They were partly right. We spent evenings in local flamenco joints, singing and dancing and knocking back sangria. We all fancied the singer and would arrange to meet him in the daytime, when he didn't quite live up to his romantic night-time gorgeousness.

One night we had a few too many jugs of sangria. I don't know how we got back to the hotel and we must have woken up half the guests with our shrieking. As we crept down to breakfast the next morning, the housekeeper was clearing away overturned flower pots and sweeping up soil that lay scattered all over the stairs. The three of us looked at each other as we began to piece back together the events of the night before, and we sheepishly took our seats at the table, trying to pretend that the misdemeanours had nothing to do with us.

Riding high: me aged four at the seaside with our friend Kanou

With Thalia on Brighton beach, 1956

Harlech holiday: Kountis, Annie, Mum, me and Dad, 1959

Dad on a mission to collect limpets, Llandanwg, 1958

Cornwall: cousin Andrew, Simos, Dad, Mum, Athenoulla and Mariou, with Sooty and me in the doorway,1964

The Beatles are coming! Me at Rhyl station, 1963

Mum's holiday, Cornwall

Dad's holiday with Simos, Cornwall

Family foraging for wild greens, Cornwall, 1964

Holidaying in Rosas, Spain. Sooty is on the left, with Jo, me and Thalia on the right, 1965

JO'S FLIGHT

In 1967, Jo lobbed a hand grenade into my parents' lives by announcing she was taking a job in Hamburg. Not Brighton, or Edinburgh, or Nottingham, although any of those cities would have been bad enough, but Hamburg – that place overseas you had to take a boat to get to, or, if you were in a hurry, a plane. Mum and Dad must have thought their world had fallen apart. Jo was their first child, the obedient one, the one who went to French school in Kensington and had graduated into a job with one of the world's richest shipowners, Costas Lemos.

All had been well in their world as far as Jo was concerned, although at 27 she was not yet married, which must have begun to worry them ever so slightly. What had got into her? No one knew, although it must have been simmering beneath the surface for some time. Jo had an independent spirit and it was surely hard for her to see friends from the Lycée take good jobs overseas with organisations such as the UN, while she was made to stay behind to work in the City, albeit for a very rich Greek. She had tried to please my parents, who didn't want her running off to some foreign country.

Although they were not your typical narrow-minded village Cypriots, Mum and Dad still believed their daughters should stay close to home and not go wandering off on their own. It took a while for them to digest Jo's news and there were more than a few family crisis meetings. They were even visited in Riding House Street by the man who would be employing Jo in Hamburg. His personal intervention was meant to reassure them that Jo would be working for a reputable company – she wasn't about to disappear into some tinpot organisation hundreds of miles away in Europe. It seems astonishing now that someone would go out of their way like that, but that's exactly what Herr Henkelbein did.

The deal was that Jo would work in Hamburg for six months, returning to the UK and her old job after gaining some valuable experience. But when the six-month deadline passed and she hadn't returned, my parents became more or less resigned to the fact that their first child wasn't coming back. For them, the other issue was that she had picked Germany. Mum was especially upset – she had lived in London through five years of war and had developed an intense dislike of all things German. That her firstborn would want to go and live among those "warmongering monsters" who a few years earlier had been dropping bombs on her family was beyond Mum's comprehension.

But for me, Jo's adventure was a dream come true. I now had the perfect excuse to legitimately get away from our parents and spread my wings, and I wasted no time in jumping on the first Lufthansa flight to Hamburg. Seventeen-year-old me was going solo and I felt very grown-up. That trip heralded a lifetime of being happy to do things on my own.

Of course, we had a great time together. Jo was renting a large room in a nice flat belonging to a woman called Frau Junge; she was like a little sparrow, a German version of Edith Piaf, but without the incredible voice. Frau Junge would have a couple of drinks in the evenings and regale my sister with her own wartime stories, including how her husband had persuaded her to have threesomes with him and a female friend. The end had seemed nigh, she said, so convention was thrown out of the window. I suspect the Junges weren't the only ones who threw caution to the wind.

What struck me in Hamburg was how formal everyone was. They addressed each other as Frau, Fräulein and Herr, even if they had known each other for years. Colleagues who were quite proper during office hours would go out drinking together at night and get completely bladdered. Would they still address each other as Missus, Miss and Mister the next day? Yes. But my sister, as an outsider, would have none of it, demanding that everyone at home and at work call her Jo, plain and simple.

Hamburg really was a lot of fun. It's a very well laid out and pretty city built around two lakes, the Binnenalster and the Außenalster. It's also where the Beatles cut their musical teeth in their early years. As a large port, it has a well-deserved reputation as a destination for sailors looking for fun, sex and sleaze; the red-light district of St Pauli is a 24-hour haven for seamen enjoying a few days on dry land. Of course, had Mum realised that the shipping office where Jo worked was close to this depravity, she would have had a fit. Dad must have had some idea, having briefly been a seaman himself, but he kept schtum, realising he would be on a hiding to nothing if he spoke out.

My parents never did visit Jo in Hamburg, which I suspect was a way of showing their disapproval. But they looked forward desperately to Jo's visits home – their daughters were what they lived and worked for. In the days before Jo's arrival, Mum would busy herself even more than usual and would plan special meals. While she was busy cooking and getting the house ready, Dad and I would head to Liverpool Street station to await Jo's train; we felt huge excitement at being reunited with her. Back at home, after Mum's predictable tears of joy, we would all sit around the kitchen table swapping tales and laughing. Then came the steady stream of friends and relatives who wanted to say hello. We lived on this high during the days we had together, until it was time to say goodbye. This was never easy, especially for my parents, and the pull they felt as Jo boarded her train back to Hamburg stayed with them until the next reunion.

To their delight, Jo's sojourn in Hamburg ended after five years and her next "posting" was to Athens – or, more precisely, to Piraeus, which for Mum and Dad was the perfect location. At last she was going to live among her own people (or theirs). Jo had been offered another job with Costas Lemos and she spent some very happy years in Greece brushing up on her language skills and getting into the way of life. My parents were thrilled because they could holiday there whenever they felt like it – they spoke about Jo to their friends with great pride, as well as great relief that she'd finally seen sense and "come home".

My sister Jo with three of her Godchildren: Theano, Chris and Chris, circa 1960

Jo and me on her balcony, Athens circa 1970

BACK TO ROOTS

To us, Cyprus was that magical place that existed alongside our lives in London. My parents talked of little else: of their families, the beauty of their village and, most of all, the land they had left behind. Jo and I listened to endless stories about how they worked the fields, the animals that helped plough them and their much-loved olive and carob trees. Names of places where they owned land – Gomarras, Paleambello, Trikateracha, Nava – became part of our DNA. We knew them without ever visiting them. Our ancestral land had belonged to our family for generations; it had been walked upon by grandparents and their parents and their parents before them. This powerful emotional connection drew me to Cyprus. It was like entering a place of dreams.

I was first taken there as an 18-month old in 1951, but of course I barely remember it. The trip was, according to my parents, a nightmare involving a ferry from Dover to Calais, a train from Calais to Paris, another train through Switzerland and via Milan to Venice, and then the boat to Cyprus. The ship called at Bari, Brindisi and Piraeus, each time taking on more passengers, and it took about eight days.

I arrived in Cyprus looking thin and wan, having rejected food and drink along the way. Mum had been distraught at my weight loss and poor Dad had been dispatched to find fresh milk every time the train pulled into a station, leading to even more distress among Mum and Jo until he made it safely back on board. Over the years, the trip assumed comedic status. We would look back on it and wonder how we managed to arrive in one piece.

It was my parents' first visit to Cyprus and to their village, Akanthou, since emigrating pre-war. It meant everything to them to take their girls home to meet the clan. They hadn't seen their families in all those years and their only way of communicating had been through letters. Sadly, it was the last time Mum would see her beloved father: Grandpa Ktori died four years later from cancer, aged 75. He was a beautiful man who wore vraga (black breeches) and had a handsome moustache – a lot of cousins have since been named after him. Our arrival in Cyprus caused untold happiness, just as our departure three months later led to great sorrow. As many people as possible packed into the old village bus to come and see us off at Limassol port. I imagine the journey back was just as awful for my parents – and with the added knowledge that we were returning to a grey, post-war London and endless years of hard work ahead.

Jo visited again with Dad in 1962 (back then we had to take separate holidays as we couldn't afford to all go together). They had a great time, with my sister rediscovering her roots and Dad basking in the bosom of his family – or, more to the point, the bosom of his land. His love for his land was fathomless. Even so, Jo was puzzled one day to see him scraping up some earth and pouring it into a piece of newspaper. "What are you doing?" she asked. "I'm taking this back to London" he said "so if I die and I'm buried there you can sprinkle my land on to my coffin."

The next time I went to Cyprus was in 1969 on the famous Anglo Akanthou trip (more of that later, too). The minute I stepped off the plane and saw my cousins lined up to greet us I knew I was home, at least spiritually. It was odd: I was a Londoner in every way, yet the power of family drew me with such force. Of course, I "knew" my uncles, aunts and cousins straight away. It didn't matter that I'd never seen them as a grown-up before, I loved them immediately and felt completely at ease with them. I had such a good time on that trip – it was a laugh a minute, as well as a feast a minute. If a Greek loves you, he'll feed you, and we certainly ate our share.

Our family lived in simple houses with beautiful Byzantine arches and courtyards. We ate outside every night in the shimmering heat, the heady smell of jasmine filling our lungs, and felt the world belonged to us. I had never experienced such a feeling of belonging – it was the polar opposite of what I felt in London, despite our extended family there. Cyprus felt like the missing link, the last piece in the jigsaw. In Cyprus we lived and socialised outside; in London we huddled around the electric fire and took a hot-water bottle to bed.

Many of the villagers had nicknames. There was Monochattalos (one pair of trousers), Monovradgis (one pair of pants) and Skattetis (Shitman). Gourchali was married to Tsakmadjies, Turkish names meaning tobacco and lighter – a marriage obviously made in heaven. I had an uncle who, living in London in the 40s, had acquired the nickname High-pa (Hyde Park) because while walking through the park one day he had found the grand sum of £5 on the ground. Overjoyed, he ran around shouting "High-pa, High-pa, my children's salvation!"

One of the drawbacks of holidaying in Cyprus as a single 20-year-old was that the village gossips would speculate you had been "brought down to find a husband". My London-born friends and I could hear them whispering on the doorsteps as we walked by: "Who's she the daughter of?" or "How old is she?" or "He's got two daughters, she must be the young one, obviously looking for a husband." It didn't bother us. We would turn into cocky Londoners and dismiss them as silly old bags. As if we would go to a remote village in Cyprus to look for a husband – and do what for the rest of our lives? Therein lies the dichotomy of the London-born Cypriot. We're neither one thing nor the other, and this division runs through our lives always.

Of course, we couldn't holiday in Cyprus without going to a wedding or two. Back then, traditional weddings lasted three days. The rituals were incredible: I remember going with cousins to a bride-to-be's house, where they were sewing the wedding mattress and covering it with the wedding sheet. It was a social event, with girls gathered around telling risqué jokes. Everything seemed to be geared towards the newlyweds' first night and a big thing was made of their impending coupling. I was surprised at how open and indiscreet they all were. It was as if the whole village was about to go along and watch.

The weddings themselves were things of beauty. The

whole village would be invited. Tables would be laid out end to end along the entire street, bearing food that family and neighbours had spent days preparing. We ate until we burst – and then it was time to get up and dance.

Everyone would take their chairs to the village square, where the band had gathered with violin, laoudo and sometimes an accordion. The happy couple performed the traditional wedding dance, and then it was the turn of the bride to dance with her bridesmaids. Next, the groom danced with his best men, of whom there were always quite a few. Somehow the men always seemed to hog the dance floor, trying to outdo each other with their swoops and leaps. After that, everyone else would pile in and dance. No one was shy. Cypriots don't do shy.

Many of the traditional dances tell a story, such as the Threbani, in which men simulate swiping a sickle to show off their skill in harvesting. The Kartzilamas is danced in pairs usually of the same sex: the women, with eyes lowered, move their hands about to show their ability in needlework, while the men leap about and do backward flips, demonstrating their masculinity and sexual prowess. The dancing is incredibly graceful as well as lusty and passionate, leaving onlookers feeling exhilarated.

On 6 August began the Paniyiri, the greatest festival of all, in which Akanthou marked the day of its church's saint, Tou Sotiros (Our Saviour). A lot of food and drink was consumed and much merriment was made over those three days. I can still hear the sounds coming from the stalls and smell the night air, heavy with jasmine and honeysuckle. It was one giant party and I wondered at moments like that why my parents had ever left. I still have a gold bracelet bought for me at the Paniyiri by my breeches-clad Uncle Sifouna (Typhoon) for £3, which was a lot in Cyprus in 1969. I treasure it, not just because it was from him, but also for its crude workmanship.

They were such lovely, carefree times. The island left an indelible mark on me – it was more beautiful than I could ever have imagined, and I've seen more stars in that canopy of a night sky than anywhere else in the world. Just five years later, when the Turks invaded Cyprus, it was as if someone had stuck a dagger in my heart and emptied out my soul.

Dad aged 16 with Grandpa Hadji-Yiannis and Aunty Helen (Dad's sister). Dad's mum had died when he was aged three and we have no photos. Cyprus, 1926

Grandpa Ktori, Mum aged 24, Grandma Elengou and Aunty Christina, Cyprus, 1937

Me aged 18 months at Grandpa Ktori's home in Akanthou, on my first visit to Cyprus in 1951. The house was demolished shortly after the 1974 Turkish invasion

Farewell photo before returning to the UK after the 1951 trip: Me with Jo and cousin Mihalakis

Farewell photo before returning to UK after the 1951 trip: Jo, Dad, Mum, cousins Mihalakis and Lulla, me, Andrew and Photis

Family dinner at the Ktori home, Akanthou, 1973. Standing: Aunty Christina with her sister, my Mum

Family at Tata Elias and Nouna Georgia's house at Akanthou, 1969, now in complete disrepair and occupied by Anatolian Turks

At the home of Aunty Helen and Uncle Liasi (High-pa), Nava, Akanthou, 1969

Uncle Liasi with his cattle at Nava, 1969

Cousin Doulla with Uncle Photis at her wedding, Akanthou

Uncle Petri (Mum's first cousin), grandson Peter, and Aunty Angelou at their home in Akanthou, 1969

Cousins Eleni, Fotoulla, Sotiris, and Eugenia with Dad, Akanthou, 1969

Cousin Mihalakis in his policeman's uniform, Akanthou, 1969

Cousin Ktori, Akanthou, 1973

Granny Elengou with Aunty Christina at Mazeri, Akanthou, 1962, with Sotiros church in the background

Granny Elengou making koulourakia (bread sticks) with granddaughter Eugenia looking on, Mazeri, Akanthou, 1962

Charlie, Michael (aka Sooty), Dad and Aunty Helen in Famagusta, 1969

Corallia, me holding her daughter Stalo, and cousin Eugenia at Chelones beach at Akanthou, 1969

ANGLO AKANTHOU AID SOCIETY

The Anglo Akanthou Aid Society, or AA, was a charity set up by my father and two of his dearest friends, Lucas Petri and Sotiris Roussou. Their initial objective was to raise enough money to build a hospital in Akanthou, as the nearest one was miles away. There was a doctor and a midwife, that was all, and it really wasn't good enough. The AA was officially registered in 1958. Dad was the treasurer, Lucas the president and Sotiris the secretary. These men had full-time jobs, but they were dedicated and committed to their cause.

Dad had Thursday afternoons and Sundays off work. During that time, when we weren't visiting relatives, we would find him poring over his AA files or deep in consultation with the committee. The AA was registered at 57 Riding House Street and its logo was two hands gripped in a handshake – the logo was drawn by my sister and the hands were mine and Sooty's. It had small beginnings, but the charity was to grow in stature and gain much respect.

Despite the AA's worthy objectives, Mum was exasperated by how much time Dad spent trying to make it work. It took him over and it took our house over, too. We really didn't have much room, but every available space was filled with AA files and paraphernalia. Mum would pull her hair out, while Dad would laugh and take another puff on his pipe (her other bête noire). During his afternoon break from work, he could be seen making his way to the Glory with files under his arm, or sometimes he would push his luck and have the committee round to ours. Jo and I would be roped into taking tea and biscuits up to the first floor, where they could be found in the sitting room under mountains of paperwork.

I don't know how they communicated, seeing as we didn't have a phone until the early 70s. The charity got off to a slow start and raising funds must have felt like pulling teeth. It was akin to begging. Most people would put money into the proverbial hat, but occasionally you would hear someone claim that the cash was going towards my sister's education. Nothing could have been further from the truth and it hurt to hear these accusations.

Funds were raised at various functions, but mainly at weddings. Dad would go around with cap in hand, trying to sell raffle tickets when he could have been relaxing with his family. In the early years, the prize was a humble bottle of whisky. Later, when more people came on board and the charity became more established, a return flight to Cyprus would be donated, or something equally substantial.

The most popular method of raising funds was a trip to the seaside. Coaches were hired and the money from the tickets would go straight into the AA coffers. These trips were always well attended and sometimes three or four coaches would be needed to take us to Hastings or Eastbourne, Southend or Brighton. People would gather outside the Glory to be picked up, and the aim was to leave by 9am. Of course, being tardy Greeks, we would be lucky to be on the road by 10am.

Once arrived, we would traipse down to the beach together, pick our spot and get on with the day's objective: eating. Cypriots aren't like the usual holiday crowd, who have sandwiches or fish and chips at the seaside. No, we ate on the beach as we ate in our own homes. Out came the tablecloth, which was laid straight on to the pebbles. Then came the food. Keftedes, dolmades, halloumi, olives, roast chicken, bread – the list was endless. Other tourists would look at us as though we were aliens (later, as teenagers, my sister and I would cringe with embarrassment). After we had eaten, it was time for a paddle. I can't remember any of the grown-ups ever actually taking their kit off and going for a swim. The only ones who did so were the children.

Then we would go foraging. As well as limpets, Dad's favourite, we would find mussels and crabs and plants such as samphire. We would fill bags with food to take back to London, to cook or pickle and eat with fish or as a meze. We must have looked very tribal, the way we sat around in circles, picking vegetation and stuffing it into carriers. But this was the early 60s, when wild food was still a bit of an unknown. If we were to do it now, I think other people would join in and enjoy the fruits of the sea, like these old Cypriot villagers had done for centuries.

After the success of the seaside coach trips, the AA committee became really ambitious and decided to charter a plane to fly all the way to Cyprus. The decision bordered on insanity and the result was predictable. This was 1969, my first trip to Cyprus since I was a baby, and the flight was to leave from Gatwick, having picked everyone up in coaches outside the Glory. The buses filled up with excitable Cypriot holidaymakers and the problems only they could bring with them. At Gatwick, getting them out of duty free was almost impossible, but eventually all the passengers were rounded up and packed on to the plane, clutching as many boxes of cigarettes and bottles of whisky as they could carry. Dad had to do a headcount – someone was missing. More delays. Dad was a saint. Getting all those Cypriots on to a plane was nothing short of a miracle.

Once we were airborne, the merriment knew no bounds. We had songs, we had food and, what's more, we had whisky! It was like a load of kids going on their first holiday. Surprisingly, the trip went well and without too many hitches. We were in Cyprus for a month and everyone had a great time with their families. The older ones vowed to return one day to spend the rest of their lives there.

When the time came to leave from Nicosia airport, Dad did another headcount. Everyone was there. "Do you have your passports?" he asked. An obvious question, but he had to ask. "But Uncle Photi," said one woman (he wasn't her uncle), "you didn't tell us we had to have our passports as well!" Poor, exasperated Dad replied: "But you had your passport on the way here, why wouldn't you have it with you on the way back?" It was no good – we had to turn the bus back. If we could have killed her and thrown her overboard we would have done, but this was 1969 and we were civilised people. Also, we'd just had a holiday and we all felt rather fab.

The Anglo Akanthou Aid Society went on to flourish and is still in existence today. There's an annual dinner dance, as well as organised trips to monasteries and other places of interest. All the money collected goes towards good causes and to people in the community who find it hard to make ends meet. When Dad and his mates retired, the headquarters were moved from Riding House Street and subsequently set up on Holloway Road in North London. The AA's current president is George Papaphotis and its members meet on a regular basis. The three founding members, all now passed away, are still honoured at official functions.

The hospital in Akanthou, however, was never built. Instead, a new primary school was constructed in the 60s. Yet, within a few years, Turkey had invaded and the school fell into Turkish hands. The Greek Cypriot children were run out of the village, becoming refugees, and were consequently deprived of education. I can't help but think of the blood and sweat of those three dear men – all the pounding of streets to raise funds, all the whispers and suspicion they endured. This is what it came to. A greater tragedy could not have been foreseen and their life's work became their personal pile of dust and ashes.

Anglo Akanthou Aid Society "beano" to Eastbourne, September 1959. I've taken my doll Jeanne-Pierette to the seaside!

Another Anglo Akanthou trip to the seaside, this time to Hastings in May, 1959

Dad, Mum, Kanou and Aunty Tinou (Helen and Lulla's mum) sunning themselves in Eastbourne, September 1959

Savva, Helen, Lulla, Jo and me, Eastbourne, September 1959

Kanou with limpets, Hastings, May 1959

GREEKS ON FILM

As if living among Greek Cypriots wasn't enough, and as if the AA didn't consume all his time, Dad had to take it one step further. He arranged, with his friend Mr Pattalis and a couple of others, to import and screen Greek films to the local community every Sunday evening, at either the Palace Theatre at Cambridge Circus or the Prince of Wales Theatre just off Piccadilly. Mr Pattalis imported foreign newspapers and videos and had friends "in the know", including some at the Greek production company Finos Films. I remember a man called Frixos, who was directly in charge of bringing these films over to the UK.

A certain frisson surrounded the screenings, particularly among our older relatives. People would gather at our house, usually Sooty with her parents, and after collecting Helen and her mum we would make our way through Soho to the theatre. Sleazy Soho, with its dark corners, its used needles, its gutters full of piss. It didn't matter – Soho was part of life, our life, and we loved it. As we got closer to the venue, we could hear the hordes of Cypriots gathered outside and making a racket as they greeted family and friends, oblivious to the perplexed non-Greeks passing by.

Parked up would be the man who sold peanuts. He was very popular. In later years we could buy koubes (stuffed meat pasties) and other small eats, but for now everyone was buying peanuts. It was almost a condition of entry that you showed a bag of nuts with your ticket. I felt sorry for the cleaners, because the floor of the theatre at the end of the performance would be covered in a sea of shells. And if the Greeks didn't buy food from outside, they would bring their own and leave the rubbish behind when they left. They loved eating and talking, and would do both all the way through the film. A perfect night out.

These were huge social gatherings and my parents looked forward to them. The whole theatre seemed to know each other. Helen and I would look out for the boys we fancied and spend most of the film gazing at them. We weren't at all shamefaced. If my current crush happened to be there, my night was made.

Lights down and the film would start. The Greeks made only two types of film, or at least that's how it seemed. There were hilarious slapstick comedies, usually starring Thanasis Veggos, and tragedies that reduced everyone to tears. Classic themes like forbidden love spawned endless films and must have kept the Greek economy going. A common storyline was: penniless country girl falls for rich spoilt boy who has a dragon of a mother. Or: spoilt rich son gets poor housemaid pregnant and she is kicked out on to the streets. Bizarrely, a musical interlude was nearly always edited into these films. The screen would suddenly switch to popular singers performing in small clubs where traditional Greek music was played. Favourites such as Stelios Kazantzis or Mary Linda would appear and then, just as suddenly, the screen would switch back to the film.

The audience would be gripped by every word, every emotion. They would cry out at injustice, sigh with grief for dying heroines and boo mothers who stood in the way of young lovers. I've never witnessed so much audience participation – it was as though their lives depended on what was happening on screen. Our mums were a typical case. They took these films very seriously, sobbing into their hankies while we London kids creased up laughing, much to their annoyance. They used to insist that these things happened in real life, didn't we know?

Films like *Golfo*, *A Girl in Black* and *Stella* (which was screened at Cannes) have now become classics. One film star in particular – and she was every inch a Film Star – had a huge following. Aliki Vougiouklaki was Greece's answer to Brigitte Bardot. She could be cute, happy, unhappy, it didn't matter – the audience loved her. She excelled in *Astero*, playing a shepherdess lover driven mad after an arranged marriage. The film represented Greece at the Berlin Film Festival in 1959, though I believe the critics were left to ponder its significance.

Of course, these films transported our parents back to the world they had left behind – one they romanticised more and more the longer they were away. They particularly loved the ones in which the characters wore traditional costume, as though this was their stabiliser in a world of unknowns: the men wearing foustanella (pleated short skirts) and sporting big, black moustaches (symbols of manhood), and the women in shepherdess garb with long black plaits (symbols of maidenhood). Our mums and dads would analyse these wretched films as they walked home. How they readjusted to their lives in the West End I'll never know, but they somehow did, until the next cinema outing.

OXFORD STREET AND BEYOND

My family lived a stone's throw from what is now one of the world's busiest shopping streets. It wasn't always thus. Back in the 50s and 60s, shopping on Oxford Street was a relatively civilised experience. The shops would close after lunch on Saturdays and reopen on Mondays; there was no Sunday trading. For something to do on a Sunday, we would promenade the length of Oxford Street, up to Marble Arch and back again, and then down Regent Street to Piccadilly, just to window shop.

My parents were careful with money, like a lot of their generation, and although they weren't stingy they preferred to save and spend money on things that would last them years. In the 80s, Dad was still wearing a coat that was at least 40 years old – he looked like a gangster in this heavy black number with wide double-breasted lapels. We were lucky that we had a few relatives who were tailors in Soho, and they made Dad's suits, sports jackets and trousers. Cousins Kyriacos and Savvas Ktori worked at Sam Arkus on Berwick Street, while George Evangelou, another cousin, had his own workshop on Meard Street. The only things Dad would ever buy – or rather, we would buy for him – were his shirts, jumpers and underwear, usually from Marks & Spencer on Oxford Street. And then there were his hats. He always wore brown fedoras from Dunn and Co, the gentlemen's outfitters on Oxford Street, now long gone.

As well as being a shopping destination attracting people worldwide, Oxford Street was also our local high street. Sure, it was where we went to buy clothes, but it was also where we got all our other bits and pieces. Our first port of call was always Bourne & Hollingsworth. Bourne's, as we called it, was a respectable middle-class department store that started out as a drapers in Westbourne Grove, and it was where smartly dressed mothers took their daughters to buy wedding dresses. I bought mine from Bourne's in 1976 and it was the first and only one I tried on.

The store had a side entrance on Wells Street, even nearer to our house than the main entrance on Oxford Street. Bourne's sold almost everything: we would drop in to buy sheets or shoe polish, stockings or thread, china cups or yards of material, perfume or stationery. There was even a wonderful dry-cleaning department on the first floor, which always returned our clothes looking pristine. The woman who ran the cleaners had wavy dark hair, red lipstick and glasses – even though the last time I saw her was probably 50 years ago, her face is still etched in my memory.

We were very sad when the store closed down in 1983. Bourne's was a smart shop with smart assistants who offered personal service. Until around the late 50s, you would be invited to settle into a comfy chair and even be offered tea and cake. Bourne's was apparently a strict employer, but fair and caring: it looked after its staff, providing accommodation for its young female workers in a hostel in nearby Gower Street. Yet, like a lot of those traditional old stores, it couldn't keep up with life in the fast lane. After its demise the building was gutted, though the facade was saved, and Bourne's was replaced by a ghastly, impersonal shopping mall.

Our other most-visited shops were Woolworths and HMV. Woolies was great – downmarket, of course, especially compared with Bourne's, but full of goods at a fraction of the price. Mum and her Cypriot friends would say they were going to "Exapenni" instead of to Woolworths, as "Exapenni" in Greek means sixpence and nothing cost more than that in Woolies in those days. This was what most London Cypriots called Woolworths until it closed down, although some did refer to it "Youllyoss", the nearest they got to the right pronunciation.

HMV (His Master's Voice) was our Aladdin's cave, a music lover's heaven. I spent hours in that shop, going through racks and racks of EPs, LPs and singles. Back then you could listen to any track you wanted by going into a listening booth: you would put on your earphones, press the appropriate button and tune in. Jo and I went to HMV every Saturday and sometimes during the week, spending most of our money on our latest favourites. She would buy Elvis Presley and Conway Twitty, and when I was nine she gave me a 78 of Cliff Richard's *Living Doll*, which I still have. I loved Cliff back then and played that record so much I eventually wore a hole in it.

In the early 60s, I would be the first to rush to HMV to buy the latest Beatles release, the Rolling Stones and anything Motown or R&B. HMV also had a great "world" section where we bought piles of Greek and French records. Mum would pull her hair out, mortified that Jo and I weren't saving our money for a dowry and our first house. As if! All my money went on music, clothes, books and travel – what teenager wanted to save for a boring old house? As it happens, I did somehow cobble together £3,000 for a deposit on a three-bedroom home in Wimbledon. The house cost £15,000, way back in 1975.

Many other shops that did good trade during the 60s and 70s have since closed down: department stores like Peter Robinson, Marshall & Snelgrove and, more recently, Dickins & Jones. Smaller places like Jays, an exquisite shop that sold antique silver and beautiful jewellery, have all disappeared. I loved the branch of Paris's Galeries Lafayette on Regent Street. I used to buy gorgeous underwear there back in the 60s, but the store closed down because the bosses thought Regent Street was going downmarket.

The saddest thing for us locals was the loss of the cinemas along Oxford Street. There were so many. Our family favourite was Screen One and Two near Oxford Circus. Screen Two was where we went to view the week's worth of news, produced by Pathé and voiced by a very plummy man who spewed out government propaganda. This was before televisions entered most homes and, unless you had a radio or bought newspapers, the cinema was the only way of catching up on world events. Screen One played cartoons over and over on a loop: Tweety Bird, Sylvester the Cat, Popeye. A gigantic aquarium was built into the wall in the main foyer and we would be mesmerised by the magical sight of the tropical fish while queueing for tickets.

Another wonderful cinema was the Academy, which stood on the corner of Oxford and Poland streets and eventually grew into Academy 1-2-3. As an art-house cinema it attracted the film buffs of the day, but sadly it closed in 1986. I remember being taken there by my sister to see umpteen films of Shakespeare plays, including Laurence Olivier's *Richard III*. During Jo's "French period" we went to Truffaut's *Les Quatre Cents Coups*, and another film I'll never forget seeing there is Ingmar Bergman's *Wild Strawberries*. It was extremely disturbing, especially for me as a seven-year-old. The scene where the coffin drops to the ground, spilling open to show a man's hand, was terrifying – almost as terrifying as the clock with no hands. In its day, Oxford Street had nine cinemas. Now there are none.

Yet there is some comfort. The screen at what was the Regent Street Polytechnic, now the University of Westminster, has been completely revamped and reopened. It's such a gem that it's hard not to shout about it from the rooftops. Back in 1896, this iconic cinema became the first in the UK to show a moving picture when it hosted a demo of the Cinématographe machine invented by the Lumière brothers. So there you go, the birthplace of cinema in the UK – who wouldn't want to go there?

The 60s were the beginning of pop culture and to be young was to rule. For me, as a teenager, it was the opening up of a whole new world. British rock music was exploding, London was the place to be and my friends and I felt a real sense of ownership. Growing up in this frenzy of sound and colour was a game changer.

New magazines were being published with content like

we'd never seen before. The brilliant *Nova* spoke to women as people rather than housewives – it was cutting-edge. Our mothers' generation was brought up on titles like *Woman* and *Woman's Own*, full of cooking recipes and stories of romance, but they weren't for us. *Nova* splashed the headline "The Big O" right across the page, at a time when it was outrageous for a magazine to talk about female orgasms. Then there was *Cosmopolitan*, which took sex and put it on the front page, and *Viva*, an erotic women's magazine published in the 70s. I recall showing a double-page spread of a male nude to Aunty Braxou when she came over to visit and she almost died of shock. She claimed she'd never even seen her husband, Uncle Polivi, naked and there I was sticking a great big penis in her face!

Fashion also changed beyond recognition. Out went the stuffy, in came the mini. Shops like Barbara Hulanicki's Biba in Kensington were phenomenal – they were so original and arrived seemingly out of nowhere. Heavy, smoky eyes were de rigueur at Biba, as well as pin-striped bell-bottomed trouser suits and gorgeous floaty dresses. When we entered its hallowed space, we felt like we were having an out-of-body experience. It was a place where the music was played so loud we could barely breathe, where girls – and boys – would drape themselves over sofas and stay there all day. It felt decadent – and that's exactly what it was.

Carnaby Street was right on my doorstep. There were only two streets where everyone wanted to shop: Carnaby Street and the King's Road. The hippies and later the mods would descend on boutiques like John Stephen, Lady Jane, Mary Quant's Bazaar and Granny Takes a Trip. Psychedelia ruled and everyone looked like they were tripping, even if they weren't. The Who, the Small Faces and the Rolling Stones would buy their "gear" on Carnaby Street and then walk five minutes down the road to record some music on Denmark Street's Tin Pan Alley, or play a gig at the Marquee in Wardour Street. Now, Denmark Street is being threatened with virtual wipeout to make way for development and the capital's new Crossrail network.

THE FOOD OF LOVE

The West End was where bands – or groups, as they were called back then – converged. You virtually tripped over musicians walking down the street. The place was changing rapidly and a lot of music and TV studios were emerging. In the mid-50s, ATV's Britallian House studios operated in Foley Street, round the corner from our house. If you stood outside on a Friday night, you would see the likes of Marty Wilde, Cliff Richard and Billy Fury making their way out of the building. Packs of screaming girls would chase their cars down the road – it was a foretaste of Beatlemania and all good fun.

I was just a kid and I was mad about Cliff. A huge moment for me was when I saw him and the Shadows leaving Britallian House one quiet Saturday morning. It was pure chance and there was no one around apart from me and my sister. I flew across the street – Jo says she couldn't see my legs, they were moving so fast – and asked for their autographs, even though I felt completely tongue-tied. I was only about eight years old and they were very sweet. I still remember what Cliff was wearing that day: a yellow towelling top, with his black quiff hanging over his eyes. I thought he was the coolest guy ever.

A few years later, the Beatles stole my heart. The first time I heard them was on the radio in 1962. Dad was a news junkie and a radio obsessive, and in our sitting room was his pride and joy, his Pye radio. It was a beautiful piece, mahogany with a gold grill over the speaker, and has now been inherited by my cousins in Cyprus. No one was allowed to touch it, unless they were polishing it, and then only if it was switched off. The Pye brought the world to Dad's ears. The problem was, it was on the first floor in the posh sitting room and most of the time we sat in the basement kitchen. After some research, Dad discovered he could run a cable from the back of the Pye out through the window and down to the basement, where it was fed through the kitchen window and into a loudspeaker. He would only need to go upstairs to turn the radio on and off. Those three flights of stairs were a labour of love.

It was via this makeshift set-up that I first heard the strains of *Love Me Do*. I was hooked. We were all hooked. All my school friends were suddenly talking about the Beatles – we couldn't believe what we were hearing.

But by 1964, I had developed a bit of a "whatever" attitude. It was local knowledge that the Beatles were filming *A Hard Day's Night* at the nearby Scala Theatre on Tottenham Street, yet I chose to ignore it. It was only when word had got around and the hysteria had gathered pace that I decided to take a look.

Sure enough, huge crowds of girls had gathered and I felt miffed I hadn't turned up before. I did manage to catch a glimpse of the band, but my friends Anne and Sandra had gone several steps further. Like me, they had known days earlier that the Beatles were filming at the Scala and they had managed to talk themselves inside – and not just once. Sandra had read somewhere that John Lennon liked baby chicks, so she'd gone and bought a couple from a pet shop to give to him as a present. I can't remember how that rather insane story concluded, but I do remember her coming out of the theatre clutching a handful of dog-ends that she'd taken from John's ashtray. I wonder if she still has them today. They would probably be worth a small fortune – a lock of Lennon's hair recently sold at auction in Germany for £25,000.

The British rock revolution was taking hold and new bands were coming through all the time. I was also mad about the Rolling Stones, who, according to my school friends, you weren't supposed to love if you loved the Beatles. That made no sense to me: good music is good music, and to have an argument over it is ridiculous. Rod Stewart's *Good Morning Little Schoolgirl* was huge for me, as was Tommy Tucker's *Hi-Heel Sneakers*. I loved the Yardbirds with Jeff Beck and Keith Relf, and the Animals with Eric Burdon's amazing gravelly voice. Later, it was all about Cream and Eric Clapton's mind-blowing guitar riffs. I was lucky enough to see Eric, aka God, at the Rainbow in Finsbury Park in the early 70s. The whole room exploded and I buzzed like a wired snake along with my partner in crime, my music-mad Godbrother Charlie.

My other partner in crime was Charlie's cousin Michael (aka Sooty – another one). In 1971, Michael and I saw Alice Cooper together at the Rainbow – he appeared on stage with kohl-rimmed eyes, long straggly hair and a live snake wrapped around his neck. It was a bizarre gig, and a great one. The problem was that it seemed to go on forever, unlike today's curfewed concerts, so we decided to stay until the last chord was struck and work out how to get home later. Afterwards, we waited for a bus to take us home. We waited and waited and waited – nothing. No buses, no trains and definitely no cabs. It wasn't so bad for me as Riding House Street was just about walkable, if you didn't mind schlepping for a couple of hours, but Michael lived miles away in Chiswick. We scratched our heads. Not much happening up there. I couldn't call my parents because they didn't have a phone and certainly didn't have a car. We also didn't want to trouble Michael's parents, who would have freaked at the thought of their only child being stranded.

In the end, we phoned a friend – a friend with a car. Andrew was Michael and Charlie's first cousin and a bit of a night owl. He was also one of my best friends. But he lived right on the other side of town in Richmond, with his parents and his brother Douglas. It was well past midnight and we hated doing it, but we were desperate so we made the call. Douglas answered, half asleep: "Hello, yes? Do you know what time it is?" "Sorry, Douglas, can we talk to Andrew please?" "*Do you know what time it is*?!" Feeling very small, we hung on, wishing the ground would swallow us up, and eventually we heard Andrew's voice – he must have thought he was having a bad dream as we explained our dilemma. Nevertheless, he got into the car and drove for miles to pick us up. By the time he arrived, dawn must have been breaking. Who else would have done that for us?

I must include some stories about Charlie, Andrew and Dad. Charlie recalls walking down Cleveland Street with his friend Arthur and two girls they had just met. At the back of Charlie's mind was a nagging worry that they would bump into my dad, his godfather. He knew Dad would be all over him like a rash, being the affectionate godfather that he was, and Charlie would be hugely embarrassed in front of the girls. Sure enough, who should he see on the other side of the road? Charlie tried to take cover, but Dad spotted him, crossing the road and giving Charlie a huge hug and a big kiss on either cheek. "Hello, dahli, how's Mammy, how's Daddy?" he asked. Charlie's credibility was shot to pieces. He would occasionally see one of the girls after that and she always asked him how his "Mammy" was.

Amazingly, the same thing happened to Andrew. Walking down Riding House Street with two girls from the architectural firm where he worked, Andrew thought he was the bee's knees. He was young, handsome, eligible and had a girl on each arm. But as he neared our house he had the same niggling fear as Charlie. Of course, who should he see coming round the corner carrying a couple of shopping bags? "Oh, dahli, haav are you?" Dad asked, putting his bags down and smacking a dirty great kiss on each of Andrew's cheeks. Andrew's ego deflated like a balloon. What on earth were the girls going to say back at the office?

Another occasion that Charlie remembers well was when Dad broke his leg tripping over something and was laid off work, his limb immobilised in plaster. Charlie, being a good godson, came to visit him at Riding House Street. The next time he called round was a few months later. This time, Dad opened the front door with his arm in plaster. Charlie did a double take: "Wasn't it your leg you broke, Tata?" "Yes, dahli mou, it was, but now I've broken my arm as well." Dad was the clumsiest of men, but also the sweetest.

Anyway, back to the music. Many other concerts were seen through a haze of drink and drugs – I happily curled up and fell asleep at the Grateful Dead at Alexandra Palace, missing the whole thing. Luckily, Charlie was there to bring me back to life and get me home. I saw David Bowie at Earl's Court in the 70s, as well as the Eagles, the Stones and Pink Floyd, who played the whole of *The Dark Side of the Moon* and were note-perfect. One man from across the Atlantic had a major impact on me. I first heard *The Freewheelin' Bob Dylan* when I was 14. It was played to me by my crush, Louis, upstairs at his parents' house on Barnsbury Road in Islington, and I was blown away. I'd never heard such lyrics before – everything he said made sense. I was a teenager trying to understand the world and Dylan spoke to me. He was outraged and I was too. He was an idealist and I was too. He was anti-injustice and anti-war – and I was too.

Louis also introduced me to the blues. The genre was more popular in the UK than in the US, I imagine because of the racism that was endemic in the States at the time. It was thanks to British pioneers like John Mayall and Eric Clapton, who backed them on club tours around the country, that we got to hear blues greats like John Lee Hooker and BB King. Sonny Terry and Brownie McGhee were two of my favourites and I was lucky enough to see them at the 100 Club. So many bands, so much music.

The Hammersmith Odeon (now the Apollo) was a treasured venue. There I saw the Beatles, the Beach Boys, Chuck Berry, Jethro Tull and Queen, who sang *Bohemian*

Rhapsody live for the first time and blew us all away. I went to gigs by Van Morrison, the Who, Santana, Talking Heads, Kraftwerk, the Pretenders and Blondie, and more recently the wonderful Rufus Wainwright and Buddy Guy. There are a lot of ghosts at Hammersmith – you can feel the past when you walk in. The walls hum with the sound of the music that has been played there. I was lucky enough to see the Beatles at both Hammersmith and Finsbury Park in the 60s – I saw them but I couldn't hear them. It's true what they say: girls screamed their heads off and drowned the music out.

What I loved about gigs back then was their shambolic nature. If the tickets said the gig was starting at 8pm, we knew we didn't have to get there until 9pm at the earliest. No one was ever on stage on time, so we would stay in the pub and stroll over when we felt it was probably about to begin. Now, it's so different. Everything starts and finishes bang on time, and tickets cost an arm and a leg.

The Beatles concert that I saw in Rhyl with my sister was a landmark event in my life, but Bob Dylan at the Albert Hall in 1966, also with Jo, came close to eclipsing it. This gig went down in history. Dylan came on with just his acoustic guitar and harmonica, and went through his repertoire of folk songs. After the interval, he came out with an electric backing band. I loved it, but many didn't and somehow felt cheated. They called him Judas and walked out. Subsequent press reviews were scathing, yet Dylan's electric period carried on despite the fans who couldn't accept change.

My taste in music was quite wide at the time and still is. We would often go and see Greek singers when they were in London. Nana Mouskouri was one of the first to come over, and others like George Dalaras, Nikos Xilouris and Maria Farandouri followed. On one unforgettable night, I went with Dad to see the Greek composer Mikis Theodorakis at the Albert Hall. Theodorakis wrote beautiful, stirring music, often translating his left-wing politics into song. Instead of being in the stalls, our seats were at the back of the stage. We were annoyed at first, especially when the orchestra came out and sat with their backs to us, but then the great man himself walked on stage and took his place at the podium, facing us directly. We realised then that we had the best seats in the house. Dad and I were in raptures: to see Theodorakis up close, to witness his every movement, gesture and facial expression, was a thrill and a privilege.

One LP that came out in 1973, just as I was holidaying in Cyprus, took the Greek world by storm. Everyone I knew loved it. It was called *Mikra Asia* and the singers were George Dalaras, Greece's answer to Bruce Springsteen, and Haris Alexiou. It was pleasure and pain: it told of the plight of the Greeks who were driven out of Asia Minor (present-day western Turkey) by the Turks in the 1920s. Each song spoke of lost friendships and lost neighbourhoods, of becoming refugees and of homes left behind. How ironic that, within a year, history would repeat itself and the songs we sang with carefree nostalgia would assume a different meaning. The 1974 invasion came and the Cypriots suffered the same fate as those Greeks in Asia Minor, losing everything to the Turks. For us, it was a bitter pill to swallow.

Tickets to ride! I saw the Beatles live in concert in 1964 and 1965

Helen and Jo in our upstairs sitting room with Dad's beloved Pye radio

Thalia and me outside flamenco music club, Spain, 1965

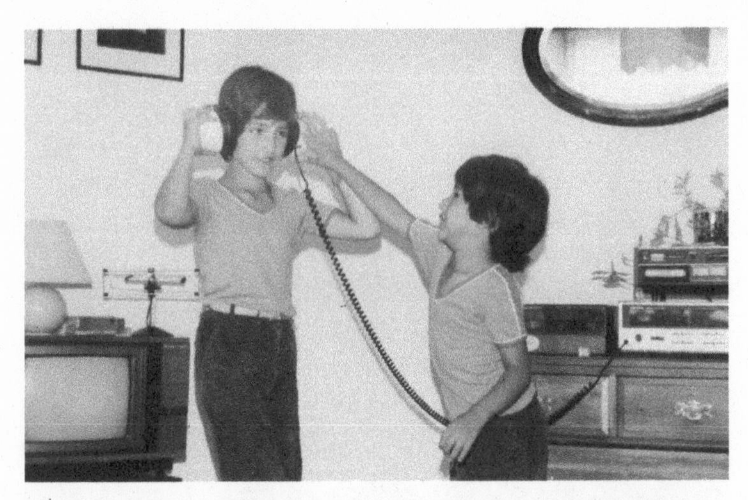

My godson Jason and his brother Nick at my house in Wimbledon, already showing a love of music, 1980

Me and Jason in Douglas and Shirley's garden on Douglas's 70th birthday, 2012

CAREER GIRL

My first love was art. I would sit at the kitchen table with pencils and a small box of paints, creating what I always hoped would be a masterpiece, and I would paint on any available surface. My marks in the subject were always good, usually top of the class, and I had dreams of going to art school. But my parents wanted me to be a teacher. They weren't happy about the idea of me joining the ranks of the "unwashed and unemployed", which was how they saw artists, and teaching was a respectable profession in their eyes. Well, there was no way I was going to be a teacher. I couldn't wait to leave school and certainly wasn't going to spend the rest of my life incarcerated in one. But I had no idea how I would use my artistic skills and, with no support from home, the whole thing eventually died a death.

Instead of going to art school, I went to secretarial college. What horror! But in my parents' eyes, it was the best thing for me. I learned to type and do shorthand while continuing with other subjects like English and French. It was a ghastly place – I can't even bring myself to name it – and the standard was very low. It made me miss grammar school and the lively, intelligent girls who went there.

After my year at the dumb factory, I got a job. It was 1967 and I joined the sales and marketing department of the publisher Collier Macmillan, located on South Audley Street in Mayfair. I answered an ad in the *Evening Standard* at the end of term, left secretarial college on the Friday and began my new job on the Monday. Finding work was a piece of cake back then.

CM occupied a beautiful Georgian house. The first floor was the domain of the managing director, Fred Kobrak, who worked in a wonderful pine-panelled room full of beautiful books and steeped in history. I enjoyed my time there very much. My walk from Riding House Street to the office took about 20 minutes: I went through the back streets and into Bond Street, where I usually stopped to buy a packet of Sullivan Powell Turkish cigarettes. They smelled divine and so different to English cigarettes, and I thought I was very sophisticated. Then it was up Brook Street, through Grosvenor Square, across North Audley Street and into South Audley Street, past the eclectic tableware shop Thomas Goode and up the steps into work.

I've almost always been able to walk to work. Living in central London meant I didn't have to ride the tube, the bus or the train from suburbia. When I think about the people who have to commute from miles away, knackered before they've even reached their desk, I realise how incredibly lucky I was. I was able to stroll through the streets and squares of London, unhurried and unstressed.

I made some great friends at CM and we never stopped

laughing. I don't recall doing much work, but we must have or the grown-ups would have pulled faces. I remember our 60s clothes, the mini-skirts and dresses – those were the days when you didn't mind being wolf-whistled. The future looked full of promise. This was also when cannabis first entered my life: the visiting brother of an American colleague had bought an enormous amount of dope with him, and he shared it with us at CM. I was really quite naive and didn't know how to smoke it, only that I wanted to. A friend came over to Riding House Street one evening and we held our small piece of dope at the lit end of a cigarette, thinking that would be enough to get us high, then spent the next hour walking around wondering if we were.

Meanwhile, the brother, who was due to return to the States, decided he couldn't leave his stash behind and swallowed the lot – all four ounces of it in one go. It's a wonder he didn't overdose. Somehow, in the middle of his meltdown, he managed to call our colleague, telling her, among other things, that the phone box was swallowing him up. He wasn't far away and she dropped everything to get to him. He was in a bad way, but he was safe, and the worst thing to happen was that he missed his flight home the next day, and the day after.

His experience put the wind up us, so we stuck to what we knew best: drinking. Friday nights were drinking nights and they were always a bit extreme. Our little group would leave work to go to the pub, the Red Lion near Curzon Street. We thought it was really nice, but we were so young we never fully appreciated just how classy it was – it was very popular with actors and I remember seeing Stewart Granger and Richard

Burton there. We would gather in one of the little booths and get completely pissed. My choice of drink back then was a sweet martini with ice and slice, a nod to my Cypriot taste for sweet things. After a few hours of solid drinking, I would somehow make my way back to Riding House Street, where Mum would be unable to work out why I looked so ill. I was just 17, with a very tender disposition, and I'm amazed I never got into any serious trouble.

The Swinging Sixties were also the era of dissent. Our sense of injustice was great. Whether the protest was pro-CND or anti-Vietnam War, we would be out on the streets with our flags and banners. Racism was rife in the US in the 50s and 60s, and we were disgusted at pictures of black people being made to sit at the rear of buses, and of segregated restaurants, theatres and even toilets. Rioting, beatings and shootings were commonplace. But the civil rights movement was gaining pace. In August 1963, a quarter of a million people gathered in Washington to hear Martin Luther King Jr give his famous "I have a dream" speech. It paved the way for serious change. Things were starting to head in the right direction, but five years later King was assassinated, killed by a single bullet while supporting striking workers in Memphis, Tennessee.

Feelings among the youth were running high. Sometimes it was like we were stewing in a cauldron of anger and discontent. I remember walking back from work in March 1968 and seeing thousands of people laying siege to the US embassy in Grosvenor Square, in one of the angriest anti-Vietnam War protests ever. "One, two, three, four, we don't want your stinking war," they cried. Mounted police were charging the crowds. I skirted the area and went home, but some 200 arrests were made that day and 50 people were taken to hospital. In May that same year, rioting students took to the streets of Paris, while strikes brought France to a virtual standstill. And then in June, Bobby Kennedy was shot dead. His death affected us badly: it was enough that his brother JFK had been assassinated in 1963, but now Bobby was dead, too.

In April 1968, Enoch Powell made his infamous "rivers of blood" speech, warning against what he saw as the dire consequences of continued immigration. It wasn't what we wanted to hear, especially in my household – my family were "foreigners", but we were hardworking and well-assimilated. As far as I was concerned we were all one people, whether we were black, white or bright pink. My friends and I were sick of political bullshit, and killings, and grown-ups telling us they knew better when they obviously didn't.

I stayed at Collier Macmillan for four years and then moved to a hotel and catering magazine on St Giles Circus, not far from Tin Pan Alley. It was the time of the hugely influential musical *Hair* and my office on the first floor was right opposite the cast's dressing room. We would often wave and shout hello to each other. *Hair* was a joyous, iconic musical, the first of its kind, and it swept everyone away with its message and optimism. Essentially political, it was a product of the hippie counterculture and explored the peace movement, drugs and the sexual revolution. The actors lined up on stage to expose themselves, emerging from under a vast sheet to stand before the audience fully naked. It was actually humbling. The songs were wonderful, too.

It wasn't just *Hair* that added colour to my life back

then. Around the corner on Shaftesbury Avenue was a little restaurant called Stavros, owned by Cat Stevens' father, who was Greek Cypriot. The family lived upstairs. I was a huge fan of Cat's and would often look out for him. One day I spotted him inside an art materials shop on New Oxford Street. I was struck dumb and, instead of talking to him, I watched as he chose some brushes and then walked out of the shop and out of my life.

My time at the magazine wasn't very happy. In fact, I hated it and made up my mind to leave as soon as I could. It took me two years to get out. After sexual advances from my immediate boss, I knew enough was enough. It wasn't as if I could go to anyone to complain – this was the 70s and his best friend was the MD, who would have laughed in my face and told me to leave if I didn't like it. I walked past the building recently and was surprised to see it is now the Cuban embassy.

After that I spent just three months at Phaidon Press on Cromwell Place in South Kensington. The building was gorgeous: white stucco with a stunning artist's studio on the top floor that was flooded with light. Phaidon produced the most beautiful books on art and design that I had ever seen, but I didn't enjoy the work. I was editorial assistant to two young women, both very nice. The book we were working on was about Giacometti and I spent my time proofreading. It's not that I don't like to read, but when confronted with hundreds and hundreds of pages of words to check, my mind goes blank. I couldn't take the minutiae of detail and so I looked for a job elsewhere. Luckily, I was offered a position at Orbis Publishing, a creative fun factory, and there I stayed for the next seven years. The original office was on Russell

Square, but in 1974, a year after I joined, we moved into a former printers on Bedfordbury in Covent Garden.

This was a troubled period in the British economy, riven by industrial action. The miners had imposed an overtime ban, with the aim of halving coal production, and later went on strike. To counter this, and to conserve energy, Edward Heath's Conservative government introduced the three-day week. Commercial consumption of electricity was reduced and we were plunged into darkness. We were allowed to use electricity for three consecutive days only, and the other two we worked by candlelight. It was very Dickensian and very weird. This lasted for three months, from January through to March 1974. A snap election was called, resulting in a hung parliament, and Heath failed to gain enough parliamentary support. He was out and so was the three-day week.

The 70s were very gloomy and everyone seemed to be striking, from gravediggers to hospital workers, firemen to Ford car workers. It seemed like everywhere you looked there were disgruntled people shouting slogans and carrying banners. On top of this there were the Troubles in Northern Ireland, with the IRA planting the occasional bomb here on the mainland. And then there was the racial tension: young black men were being randomly stopped in the streets by police using the "suspected person" law as an excuse. The sus law allowed them to stop, search and arrest anyone they thought was acting suspiciously.

In the midst of this, in the summer of 1974, the Turks invaded Cyprus after a short-lived coup by Greek Cypriot right-wingers intent on union with Greece. I didn't want this to affect my work, I really didn't, but I couldn't help feeling angry, especially at my British colleagues and friends. How could they carry on enjoying life when my family's world was being torn apart? Completely irrational thinking, of course, but they were irrational days and these people were in my firing line. I was aggrieved at the British government, which was guarantor of the island's sovereignty but seemed to be turning a blind eye. In fact, three guarantors were put in place after Cyprus gained independence from Britain in 1960: Turkey, the country that invaded; Greece, small and ineffectual; and Britain, which had bases on the island and could surely have helped, or so I thought.

Despite this period of unhappiness and unrest, there was a small chink of light in my darkness. The Covent Garden area had just been saved from demolition and it was a good time to be working there. Small independent shops were opening up, as well as cafes and restaurants. There was a real buzz and the area attracted a lot of visitors – both a good thing and a bad thing, as before too long Covent Garden was teeming with people. Still, the place was alive, full of fresh ideas, and being there you felt part of the "it" crowd. One of the restaurants, Joe Allen's, was very popular among actors and theatregoers. I was there one evening when all the customers fell into a reverential hush, and I looked up to see Elizabeth Taylor wafting past. She was acting royalty and I remember thinking how stunningly beautiful she looked.

Getting to Orbis was probably my best walk through London. I would leave Riding House Street at around 9am and head south, crossing Oxford Street into Soho. Then I'd go down Wardour or Berwick Street and cross Shaftesbury Avenue into Chinatown. Early morning was the best time to walk through Soho. The place would barely be awake. The occasional waiter would throw a bucket of water on to the pavement to wash away the previous night's excesses, while a few bleary-eyed people sat in cafes. From Chinatown I'd head into one of the little side streets, past the theatres and Sheekey's restaurant and through Cecil Court, which is full of antiquarian bookshops. Finally, I would cross to St Martin's Lane by the theatre there and head up New Row into Bedfordbury. As I write this, I'm struck by how very lucky I was to experience this every day.

Orbis was a great place to work. It published beautiful books and also partworks, those weekly magazines that build into encyclopedias. That was my department and I worked for a bright, cheerful man called George McVicar. He and his wife, Tricia, who was also at Orbis, became lifelong friends. Then there was clever Mike Joyce, our marketing manager. He had previously worked in Athens for one of the top advertising agencies and had a good handle on Greek. So much so that he'd come up with one of the best catchphrases I've ever heard in Greek: "Naha mia Yamaha", which means "If only I had a Yamaha", the Japanese motorbike. Of course, you've got to understand Greek to appreciate the sublime symmetry of that slogan. It's perfect.

We were one big, generally happy family. There was hardly a lunchtime when we didn't go out and spend a couple of hours having fun, either at the Italian restaurant round the corner or at the pub. Everyone found the time to have a laugh and also finish their work. On the occasions when I stayed at my desk with a sandwich, George would come back from his favourite restaurant, the Ivy (pre-celeb days), with a doggy bag for me containing the fillet steak he had barely touched. They knew George well there, and whenever I phoned to make a booking they always checked to see if he would like his usual. "Yes please, Puligny-Montrachet, on ice."

While I was at Orbis, I met someone who would later change my life dramatically. Audrey arrived as a temp and we worked together on the launch of one of our partworks. When things quietened down she left, and her next job was with a TV news agency, UPITN (United Press International Television News), which later became WTN (Worldwide Television News). Audrey and I kept in touch. After a year, she phoned to say she'd mastered her job on the news desk and was seeking a promotion to the scripts desk. The deal was that she had to find a replacement – and in her eyes, the replacement was me.

At first I didn't want to know. I didn't want to work shifts, weekends or Christmas Day, thanks very much. Yet Audrey persisted and I began to warm to the idea. My marriage to my first husband, Edward, was falling apart and I felt I needed a change, so I went for an interview and was offered the job – as simple as that. It was on the day that Anwar Sadat, the president of Egypt, was assassinated and I walked into a newsroom that was spinning on its head. I stood at the door and took it all in. It was then I knew that I would be leaving publishing and entering this crazy world of intense pressure, deadlines and utter exhilaration.

WTN's offices were on the fifth floor of the ITN building on Wells Street, moments from Riding House Street. They were also two floors down from the ITN bar. I was still new to the world of journalism and was aghast at the copious amounts of alcohol being drunk, not just in the bar but also in the newsroom. Pint after pint would be carried downstairs to be consumed on late shifts. The old hacks would get as drunk as skunks; carpets, desks and filing cabinets were stained with beer spilled by shaky hands. And when they'd had enough of the ITN bar, they would retire to the Crown and Sceptre on Foley Street, or the Septic, as we called it. That pub became WTN's second home a few years later, after we moved into offices opposite it – another gift to the bacchanalian hacks. I was living in my marital home in Wimbledon at the time, but now I was back in my old hood and loving every minute of it.

My life over the next decade took many turns. I met Ross, an Australian journalist, at WTN and together we made a new life. We dipped in and out of Oz, bought a flat in Maida Vale, came back to work in London every now and then, and eventually ended up on the news desk at ITN in 1984. It felt like the whole country was on a knife edge. The miners were on strike again, this time in a bid to prevent pit closures, but were eventually defeated by the Thatcher government. Our brave film crews had plenty to cover: shocking scenes of violent clashes between police and miners, and between picketing miners and working miners, were the norm. The dispute was nasty and lasted a year. It decimated whole communities and resulted in the closure of most of the country's collieries.

My career, amid all this, took off. It was a great experience working at ITN during the 80s, when money was no object. You could throw cash at a story back then without first having to get approval from the accountants, as is the case today. The newsroom was loud and exciting and we got results, with big stories like the Falklands War, the 1987 hurricane and Live

Aid defining the decade. Even with no formal training, it was possible to do well in journalism – with a lot of effort. If you have a nose for it you're halfway there. It's possible that growing up in the West End made me streetwise, and certainly that Cypriot self-belief plus some political nous gave me the confidence I needed.

There was one downside, though: I was working in the same newsroom as the correspondent Michael Nicholson. Years earlier, Nicholson had made my blood boil with rage during one of his reports. He had been sent to Cyprus in 1974 to cover mounting turmoil following a coup d'etat on 15 July. The story goes that on the day of 20 July the press pack had got wind of something big happening somewhere and had rushed off to check it out. Nicholson, to his intense irritation, was rooted to the spot, his car having just broken down. However, he was about to get a major scoop. As he stood fuming, he looked up to see the first Turkish paratroopers coming in to land on the island. He walked up to them and introduced himself with the famous line, "Hello, I'm Michael Nicholson, ITN. Welcome to Cyprus." I don't think there was one Greek Cypriot watching the ITN news that night who didn't want to lynch him.

Thankfully, I didn't have a great deal to do with him. I worked mostly on the home desk, making sure we got TV coverage of the stories of the day, setting up interviews, assigning reporters and arranging links. I would be at work by 7am, picking up toast and coffee for me and the news editor, and then getting straight down to work. We would set up the day ahead of the 10am meeting, an important gathering of news editors, producers and bulletin editors, who would discuss the day's events with the head of news and decide how and what to cover. Then everyone would traipse back to the newsroom and the pandemonium would begin. Like most newsrooms it was a huge, noisy, open-plan space. You could shout across to your colleagues without having to get up from your desk, saving vital seconds. There was a lot of laughter: we were like one big family all working towards a common goal. There was also a lot of smoking, endless smoking – we never seemed to stop.

And we never seemed to stop partying. The adrenaline coursing through our veins after working flat out had to be spent, and this was mostly in Wolsey's, the wine bar opposite, and at nearby restaurants. Many of us worked shifts, knocking off after 11 hours (if there were no breaking stories), by which time you were ready to let your hair down. There were endless tales of bad behaviour: of plates of spaghetti being shoved down trousers as a drunken bet; of cameramen falling asleep in the wine bar toilet and being locked inside overnight, giving rise to the famous tabloid headline "Booze at Ten".

One incident had us in stitches and it had nothing to do with news. I'd received a call telling me Dad was in reception. My parents still lived over the road in Riding House Street, and it was lovely to see them often, but nevertheless I thought it strange that Dad was downstairs and I hoped they were OK. Hurrying to reception, I saw Dad wearing his silly grin and holding a plate in his hands. "Your mum's just cooked these and she thought you might like some," he said as he uncovered the still-warm keftedes. "Dad, I'm at work!" I cried. God, this is ITN, I thought – what will they think of me? But my colleagues thought it was sweet, especially after I handed the keftedes round. You can never stop a Greek mum being a Greek mum and making sure her family is fed and watered, no matter where they are.

In the 90s, after my time of wandering the globe, I came back to live in the West End. Mum had died and left her flat in trust for me and Ross, from whom I'd since separated. This was an ex-council flat on Carburton Street, a leafy, pedestrianised road just off Great Titchfield Street and close to the GPO Tower. The flat was about five years old at the time and I lived there for the next decade, happy to be back in my old stomping ground in the middle of London.

It was a sad day when I left – the only time I have ever cried leaving one of my homes. The flat was the last tangible link with Mum and I hated saying goodbye. By then I had met Tim, my husband, and we pooled our money and bought a place on Hallam Street, near Great Portland Street. We were there for three years. It was a great flat on the sixth floor, art deco with fabulous parquet flooring. It even had a terrace.

Ours was the only flat in the block with outside space and we took advantage of it. Our neighbours had other ideas, however, and would ask us to be quiet if they heard us talking past 11pm. I could understand this and we were quite vigilant, but there were other problems that in the end made us think of selling up. The lift kept breaking down and having to climb up to the sixth floor, at times with several bags of food, became an enormous pain in the backside. Worse still were the upstairs neighbours. They were students from Hong Kong who would get home at around 1am, start up a drum machine and talk at the tops of their voices for what seemed like hours. They sounded like cats on heat, and I would lie in bed getting angrier and angrier until the red mist descended. I'd charge upstairs to hammer on their door: "For God's sake, keep your voices down! Can't you understand we're trying to sleep?" Their response would floor me: "But we are students." I still can't work that one out.

We tolerated this for a while, but then came the day when I picked up a brochure delivered by one of the local estate agents. Inside, a neighbour's flat was being advertised for sale at an extortionate price. I thought it was a mistake and phoned the agent to check. "Do you want to buy it?" they asked. "No, I was just checking. I live next door. Er, can you come over and value mine, please?"

Within three weeks our flat had sold. Out of the blue, we decided to move away from London. Our lives made us feel like hamsters on a wheel – we felt trapped inside our concrete citadel, needing to breathe some air. There we were in this big, beautiful city, but we seemed to do nothing more than operate in our own ghetto. We would go to work, eat at the local Italian and go shopping for food on Marylebone High Street. That was it.

So we moved to Suffolk, to a 500-year-old house in a little town full of history and nice people. Some of them are even cool! I think of Suffolk as going back to the land – I couldn't get away from the connection to the earth that was so instilled in me by my parents. I think I have the best of both worlds now, and I also know my future can't take my past away from me. Funnily enough, most of our neighbours are ex-Londoners and I do more in the city now than in the last few years of my life there. We go to the Smoke for long weekends, or take the train and meet friends for lunch. Apart from my

70s heyday, when I practically lived inside the Hammersmith Odeon, I've seen more live music in London in the past few years than ever before.

As an almost-postscript there is this. Down the road lives a woman who works for the BBC in London and has a pied-à-terre in, of all places, Riding House Street. The woman opposite her also has a flat in London – guess where? Yes, Riding House Street. It's kind of freaked me out.

It doesn't end there. Years ago, when I was at WTN, I worked with the journalist John McCarthy, who was later kidnapped and held hostage in Beirut for five years. I'd thought about him after his release in 1991, but had never tried to make contact – and in any case, I was living in Australia at the time. Fast-forward to our move to Suffolk in 2007. We were told not only that John was now based in the same town, but that he was living just five doors away. I made contact. He was our first visitor, arriving on the doorstep with his delightful daughter Lydia, then only 18 months old, and a bottle of champagne. I was completely overwhelmed. It was a magical and emotional moment, one I'll never forget.

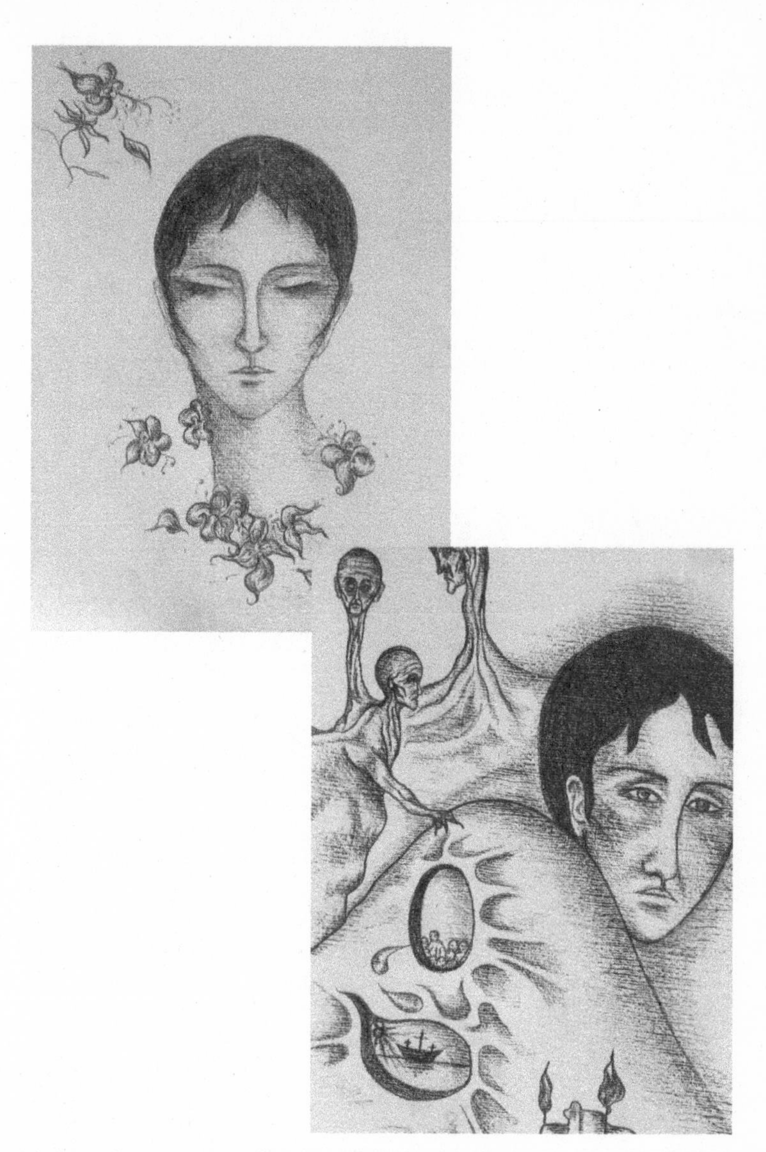

A few of my teenage sketches

Sooty posing in my bedroom with photos from 60s magazines, mainly from *Nova*

My Orbis colleagues Mike Joyce and David Breed outside a favourite watering hole, 1970s

With my favourite publisher boss, George McVicar and my good friend, his wife Tricia

The ITN news desk in Wells Street in the 1980s

ITN Chief News Editor, Nigel Hancock, perusing the papers

The Crown and Sceptre on Foley Street, a favourite watering hole for journalists in the area

Me with John McCarthy in sunny Suffolk

THE F WORD

Before winding up, I have a confession to make: I don't like the name Fitzrovia. I think it sounds a bit twee. To me, it's always been the West End and always will be. But for now let's compromise and call it the F word.

The F word apparently first appeared in print in the 40s. It's an obvious reference to the local place names: Fitzroy Square, Fitzroy Street, the Fitzroy Tavern. Many artists, writers and bohemians have hung out there over the years and many famously drank there, like Dylan Thomas, Augustus John and George Orwell. And Peter O'Toole, who Tim and I saw one night propping up the bar, looking as handsome and as raffish as ever.

The beautiful Fitzroy Square is the location for many a TV period drama – its 19th-century proportions are the perfect backdrop. One of the grand houses on the square was recently used in the film *Phantom Thread*, starring Daniel Day-Lewis and set in the glamorous post-war 50s. It showed Robert Adam's neoclassical architecture at its finest.

The F Festival first hit the streets (namely Charlotte) in 1973 and is celebrated to this day. Despite my dislike of the name, I went to the festival every year until the early 80s, when I disappeared to Australia. It was a fun event and I'm sure it still is. There was music and food and entertainment. The local restaurants, mainly Greek and Italian, would set up stalls along the street and everyone would help themselves. This included the legendary Anemos restaurant and the Mandra down the road.

Anyone who has ever been to the Anemos will not have forgotten what a wild place it was. Seared in our memories are the most vivid nights of bacchanalian revelry. I've rarely seen such excess: hundreds of plates were smashed every night, while people danced on tables and on the bar. I had my hen night there in 1976, and my sister and I got so drunk that one of the waiters walked us home – he couldn't trust us to make it back safely in the state we were in.

Once, a PA from ITN who had gone to the Anemos with colleagues dropped dead as she sat at the table. No one took a blind bit of notice. They thought she was drunk, but the poor woman had choked on her food. Her head slumped on to her plate and stayed there until it was time for everyone to go home. When they couldn't wake her up, they realised something dreadful had happened and, pissed out of their heads, they had to somehow deal with the surreal situation. A sobering lesson if ever there was one, and one I'm sure they've never forgotten.

Since those days, the area has been gentrified. There are some great new restaurants and property prices are off the scale. I think more and more people are realising that you can live as well as work right in the middle of London – if you have the money, of course. But I despair over the countless "luxury" flats that are going up, in particular those properties sold off-plan to anonymous overseas buyers who use them to stash their cash. The F word is the marketing man's ideal description for the area, and it's a gift for estate agents, too. It's sometimes even called a "village". Well, a village is a community where neighbours know each other and look out for each other. When I was growing up, our lights were on every night. Now I look at Pearson Square and wonder what the F has happened to the place. There aren't many lights on there now, and not too many neighbours hanging out of their windows wanting to chat either.

Aerial view of Fitzroy Square, not far from Riding House Street

57 Riding House Street today

Ghost sign. Part of Riding House Street was once known as Union Street

AND IN THE END

I wrote this book as a tribute to my parents, so they would not be forgotten. Those who were close to them can understand this, I'm sure, but they would probably say I needn't have written a book for Mum and Dad to be remembered. Yet I felt it was important to chronicle their lives as early migrants to London, and to record how they nurtured not only their daughters, but also their huge extended family. I know how much they were both respected for their honesty, loyalty and kindness.

Mum and Dad were certainly a good match. Their hard lives would have been enough to finish off most people, but they kept going, always counting their blessings and always saying "it could be worse". Their lifelong incentive was the thought of retirement in their village in Cyprus – for my father, that would have been in 1975.

What a cruel twist of fate, therefore, that in 1974 their world was turned on its head. Everything they had worked for was suddenly taken away from them. After an Athens-backed coup aimed at uniting Cyprus with Greece, Turkey dispatched its warships and invaded the island on the pretext of protecting the Turkish Cypriot minority. What unfolded was a huge emotional trauma for all the people of Cyprus, Greeks and Turks. The Turkish army took the northern third of the island and in effect partitioned it along what is known as the Green Line. The Turkish Cypriots, under their army's protection, were moved north, leaving behind their homes and land, and told to take over houses belonging to the Greek Cypriots. Since then, alien Turks from Anatolia – people even the Turkish Cypriots want little to do with – have been shipped in to the north to boost numbers. There were casualties on both sides, military and civilian. Some 5,000 Greeks were killed, while more than 800 Turks perished.

The Greek Cypriots stayed in their homes for as long as they thought safe, but in the end were forced to flee, with many of them heading south towards the relative safety of the British bases. For my own family, it was the end of the world they knew. Three of my cousins were taken prisoner and sent to Adana in Turkey, where they experienced conditions that were worse than inhumane, later telling of dead mice in their soup and having to resort to drinking their own urine. They were released after six weeks, perhaps because two of them had been born in London and held British passports. The third cousin was thrown in as a goodwill gesture.

The majority of the population of our village of Akanthou ran to the fields, leaving everything behind, their donkeys still tethered to their posts. God knows those animals must have suffered, too, dying a slow death for sure. For my aunts, uncles and cousins – Georgia was only three months old –

countless days and nights were spent waiting in open fields in the blistering July heat. They had no possessions and very little food. They had become refugees, another statistic in a world immune to such tragedies.

I will never forget the morning of 20 July 1974, when Mum stood at my bedroom door giving me the news that was to change our lives forever. "Egaman invasion i Tourji," she said. "The Turks have invaded." There have now been more than 40 years of diplomatic talks, with no solution to the "problem". The refugee Greeks have mostly done well for themselves: some emigrated, but most got back on their feet with help from the government. My relatives have scattered across Cyprus and live in "refugee" homes built in areas that were initially designed as camps. They are doing OK and they see each other often. The old wounds are healing with time, but they are always there, just under the surface.

For my parents back in the UK, it was the end of everything. They had lost their ancestral home and, more importantly, their land – their "mali", that thing that was part of them and drove them on while they were away from it. In their eyes, they had lost our inheritance. My mother could never stomach it. You could say it was the end of their migrant dream and they questioned the years they spent slaving in restaurant kitchens and sitting bent double on a tailor's stool. It was unbearable to see this happening to them, to see how helpless they had become.

We spent so many days and nights glued to the radio waiting for some news, any news; so many hours poring over newspapers to see if our missing boys had been found; so much time hoping against hope. And to this day there has been nothing but a lot of hot air and endless handshakes. As I write, negotiations have reached an impasse over the number of Turkish troops remaining on the island. There's also the (not so small) matter of gas deposits found in southern waters off Cyprus, with Turkey claiming half of any revenue derived belongs to the Turkish Cypriots. How this will play out is anyone's guess.

Mum and Dad were forced out of Riding House Street in 1978 when their new landlord wanted to sell. They were given a flat by Westminster Council in Lisson Grove, a rough neighbourhood, which cut them off from their beloved West End and their friends there. Dad used to say he felt like a prisoner. After he died in 1989, Mum was moved into the lovely one-bedroom flat in Carburton Street. She lived there, happily back in the West End, for the last years of her life.

My parents died in London, three years apart and both aged 78, but we decided to bury them in Cyprus. It's what they would have wanted, but alas not exactly where they would have wanted, in their village cemetery. That cemetery, for the record, has been desecrated, we presume by the invading Turkish army – and in any case it's in "occupied territory" and we wouldn't have been allowed to bury Mum and Dad there. No, they now rest in the south of the island, in a Greek cemetery where orange and lemon trees, jasmine and bougainvillea lean gently over the graves and the smell of burning incense is ever-present. Jo even found that scrunched-up piece of paper containing soil from Dad's land – it was tucked away in the back of the wardrobe – and his wish to have it sprinkled over him was granted. There is room enough in the family plot for my sister and me, should we wish to be buried there. I'm not sure if it's what Jo wants, but I do. That's where I'll be heading when the time comes. It could be worse.

«Τζι ούλλος ο κόσμος τζι αν χαχεί
Της Κύπρου μη κακόν της
Γιατί πατώ το χώμαν της
Τζιαι πίννω το νερόν της.»

– Verse by Kemalis, Cyprus

And if all the world should perish
God forbid it's Cyprus
For I walk upon her soil
And I drink her water

Cousin Sotiris, aged 17, while a prisoner of the Turkish army in 1974

The desecrated cemetery of Ayia Fotou, where my grandparents, Uncle Michael and other family members are buried, 2010

Grandpa Ktori's desecrated headstone

Uncle Michael's desecrated headstone

Me inside the desecrated church of Ayia Fotou in Akanthou, 2010

The imposing church of Chryssosotiras in Akanthou, now a mosque, 2010

Turkish flags carved into the Kyrenia range of mountains. This reminder of the 1974 invasion greets Nicosia's inhabitants every day

UNITED NATIONS  NATIONS UNIES

POSTAL ADDRESS—ADRESSE POSTALE: UNITED NATIONS, N.Y. 10017
CABLE ADDRESS—ADRESSE TELEGRAPHIQUE: UNATIONS NEWYORK

REFERENCE: PO 210 PI (S/NC) 1975

18 April 1975

Dear Sirs,

I wish to acknowledge receipt of your letter of 10 March 1975, which you addressed to the Security Council on behalf of the 16th Annual Conference of the Anglo-Akanthou Aid Society, concerning the situation in Cyprus.

As I am sure you are aware, the question of Cyprus has been recently considered by the Security Council. A copy of the resolution adopted by the Council on 12 March is enclosed for your information.

Please be assured that your letter will be dealt with in accordance with established procedures as laid down in the Appendix to the Provisional Rules of Procedure of the Security Council.

Yours sincerely,

Director
Security Council and
Political Committees Division

The Secretariat
The Annual Conference of the
Anglo-Akanthou Aid Society
57 Riding House Street
London W.1, United Kingdom

Letters from the UN Security Council sent to the Anglo Akanthou Aid Society at Riding House Street, in reply to concerns over the Turkish invasion of Cyprus. Second letter on following page.

UNITED NATIONS

SECURITY COUNCIL

Distr.
GENERAL

S/RES/367 (1975)
12 March 1975

RESOLUTION 367 (1975)

Adopted by the Security Council at its 1820th meeting on 12 March 1975

The Security Council,

Having considered the situation in Cyprus in response to the complaint submitted by the Government of the Republic of Cyprus,

Having heard the report of the Secretary-General and the statements made by the parties concerned,

Deeply concerned at the continuation of the crisis in Cyprus,

Recalling its previous resolutions, in particular resolution 365 (1974) of 13 December 1974, by which it endorsed General Assembly resolution 3212 (XXIX) adopted unanimously on 1 November 1974,

Noting the absence of progress towards the implementation of its resolutions,

1. Calls once more on all States to respect the sovereignty, independence, territorial integrity and non-alignment of the Republic of Cyprus and urgently requests them, as well as the parties concerned, to refrain from any action which might prejudice that sovereignty, independence, territorial integrity and non-alignment, as well as from any attempt at partition of the island or its unification with any other country;

2. Regrets the unilateral decision of 13 February 1975 declaring that a part of the Republic of Cyprus would become "a Federated Turkish State" as, inter alia, tending to compromise the continuation of negotiations between the representatives of the two communities on an equal footing, the objective of which must continue to be to reach freely a solution providing for a political settlement and the establishment of a mutually acceptable constitutional arrangement, and expresses its concern over all unilateral actions by the parties which have compromised or may compromise the implementation of the relevant United Nations resolutions;

75-05232 /...

Mum and Dad on their 50th wedding anniversary, 1989

Keeping the folks clean: me sweeping Mum and Dad's grave, Larnaca, 2010

ACKNOWLEDGEMENTS

I'd like to thank my sister, Joanna, and my friend Helen Pantelides for ploughing through early drafts of this book and for their much-appreciated suggestions. Thank you, too, to Douglas and Andrew Alexiou for clearing up a few facts and for their invaluable input, as well as Charlie Kounoupias for his help, his knowledgeable guidance and his excellent memory. Also to Nick Kounoupias for his expert advice. Grateful thanks to Sooty Petri, Lulla Stouppa, Mike Nolan and Nigel Thomson OBE, for putting me straight, and to Mick Stavri, Mattheos Mattheou, George Petri, Vassilis Pikkou and George Georgiou for gifting me with their humorous recollections. My appreciation to Sue Bennett for being there at the beginning and Deborah Nash for her early steer. Thanks also to Elena Ioannidou from the Greco Project, Nicosia, for her contribution of the Cypriot verse. To Jason for introducing me to his Uncle Chris at Tims Dairy and for his help – and delicious yoghurts! Huge thanks to Moira Alexiou for her early proofreading of these pages and for her corrections and suggestions. I owe a massive thanks to my editor, Isla McMillan, whose creative as well as critical eye has transformed this book into what it is today. I am eternally grateful. Last but not least, I thank my husband, Tim, for his immense support, his help and his patience throughout this deeply personal project.

If my recollections are not the same as yours, forgive me. Memories can sometimes play strange tricks and by their very nature are always personal. And lastly, if I've omitted mentioning you, I apologise. Please don't feel aggrieved – I owe you a lot, too.